The Yellow Six

James Clarke

Illustrated by Julie Clarke

BREWIN BOOKS

First published by Penguin Books 1995

This edition published by
Brewin Books Ltd, 56 Alcester Road,
Studley, Warwickshire B80 7LG in 2006
www.brewinbooks.com

© James Clarke 1995 & 2006

All rights reserved.

ISBN 1 85858 275 X

The moral right of the author has been asserted.

A Cataloguing in Publication Record
for this title is available from the British Library.

Typeset in Plantin
Printed in Great Britain by
SupaPrint (Redditch) Limited.

For

Richard Steyn

CONTENTS

Foreword	ix
Preface	x
Preface	xi
Introduction	1
Author's Note	2
Making a Bob or Two	7
Wartime and Sex Problems	11
The Great Escape	14
How a Dog Can Teach Leadership	17
The Yellow Six - The Cast	20
Yellow Six to the Rescue	23
The Secret Role of the Silver Ball	27
The Shelter the Germans Never Found	32
The Power of Observation	34
The Last Elephants in England	39
Trailing Behind Felicity	42
The Art of Smiling While Whistling	46
Twenty-four Good Deeds in One Tiny Coin	48
The Girls of St John and How to do the Twist	51
Being Nice to the French	54

The Art of Preparing Chitlings	57
Fanyana and the Bananas	60
The Day the Beasleys' House Caught Fire	64
The Mother of All Fires	67
Fenning's Fever Cure	71
Dancing and Looking After One's Own Chitlings	74
How the Spring was Sprung	77
The Grand Prix	81
The Olympiad	84
The Gang Show	86
The Scout Knife and More Little Old Ladies	92
The End of Everything	95
Acknowledgements	98

FOREWORD

By LORD LOGENBERRY OM, PC, GCMG, KCB, CBE; Chairman of the Federation of Souvenir Teaspoon Collectors' Clubs; Vice-President of the Bring Back Hanging Society; Patron of the Badger Liberation League.

My Dear Clarke,

I must insist that you stop writing to me and, again I must ask you to accept, once and for all, the fact that until you first asked me to write a foreword for your book, The Yellow Six, I had never heard of you or your wartime silver paper collection, or the Yellow Six. Nor was I ever Chief Scout of Great Britain. Bearing these factors in mind I must, once again, ask you to understand that it would be totally inappropriate for me to write a foreword for your book - in fact it is out of the question. I hope I make myself clear.

I (once again) return your manuscript herewith, please find.

It occurs to me that you may be mistaking me for Lord Cranberry.

Logenberry

PREFACE

By Lord Cranberry, KT, PC, GCVO, GBE, MC; Chairman of the Royal Bean Commission.

My Dear Clarke,

I can see no earthly reason why I should write a preface for your book and please desist from requesting that I do so. I have told you three times that I was never Chief Scout of Great Britain and Ireland and why Logenberry should have put you on to me is beyond my mental resources to fathom.

I asked my secretary to ascertain whether anybody with a name resembling mine was with the Boy Scouts Association and he tells me there was a Sir Reginald Black-Berry. Fortunately, for Sir Reginald, he has been dead many years.

Yours truly,

Cranberry

PREFACE

By Lady Margaret Black-Berry, Doncaster.

My Dear Mr Clarke,

How nice of you to write to me as the widow of the late Sir Reginald Black-Berry MC, who was, as you so cleverly recalled, Assistant District Commissioner of the Boy Scouts. This was in Bulawayo, Rhodesia, a country which, I am told, has since changed its name. What is happening to the world?

You want me to write a book for you about the Yellow Six and silver paper. I forget when my late husband was in the Boy Scouts (it was in Rhodesia, you know?) but it was certainly before 1938 because Reggie (we called him Reggie because his first name was Reginald) was dead from that year onwards - trampled by a large herd of elephants (I seem to remember). As you can imagine, we all felt a bit flat after that. But, I said to myself, 'Life must go on'. As indeed it did. I remarried the following week.

We were in Rhodesia, you know? It is now called something else. But, that's Asia for you. Ever since we gave away India things have gone from bad to worse.

I don't recall Reggie (my husband) collecting silver paper to make aeroplanes in the Second World War. Are you sure about this? He was dead, you know? He was run over in Rhodesia. I don't recall the Second World War very clearly. Was that the one with Mr Churchill in it? I recall King George. Reggie knew King George. Are you sure it was not King George who collected silver paper? Memory does funny things, you know?

I don't recall Sir Reginald Black-Berry at all. I think he has passed on. I have enclosed some silver paper as requested, please find.

Yours, etc,

Margaret

INTRODUCTION

Excuse me, Sir. May I introduce myself? I am James F Clarke, former L*E*A*D*E*R of the Yellow Six patrol of the 1st Streetly Boy Scouts; author, journalist, keen train spotter, honorary member of the Institute of Solid Waste Management; twice nominated as Solid Waste Man of the Year, and who, as a Boy Scout during World War II, collected silver paper from which to make Spitfires and Hurricanes and...
What?
I said the name's James F Clarke, former...
What?
CLARKE!
Oh. How do you do?
Fine thank you.

AUTHOR'S NOTE

No decent book is without an Author's Note. This is usually an obsequious piece of writing apologising for having had the temerity to write the book in the first place and craving the (dear) reader's indulgence for the book's shortcomings and adding some pretty wet sentiments about the author's family and upbringing in a district so poor that the municipal refuse trucks, instead of coming to take rubbish away, used to make deliveries.

By contrast, my unpretentious Note serves only to apprise you (dear reader) of the setting against which the actions contained herein, please find, took place.

It will be useful for you to know that the village of Streetly, where most of the events described in this book happened, straddles the border of Staffordshire and Warwickshire in the English Midlands. The village sits on the edge of Sutton Park, a vast natural heath of gorse and heather dappled by birch woods, silver lakes and black, glutinous marshland.

The main part of the village is a short string of shops, all on one side of Thornhill Road (the park being on the other), and a quaint little railway station. At the east end of the village are concentrated some fine mansions belonging to some of Britain's wealthiest entrepreneurs. At the much higher western end, three kilometres away, below Barr Beacon, live people of modest means (i.e. broke, one week to the next).

As English tradition dictates, a noisy highway, the Chester Road, runs clean through where most people live. At night the rumble of

Author's Note

traffic jiggles people's teeth in their bathroom tumblers; during the day the cat flattening flow of lorries is ceaseless.

Nothing has ever happened in Streetly. At least, not since Cromwell slept in Besom House, a four century old cottage opposite our house in Foley Road at the village's western end. Even then, I suspect, nothing happened. But, for a time, during World War II, the scene was enlivened by the presence of a Boy Scout group known as the Yellow Six of which I - and I say this in all humility - was the L*E*A*D*E*R.

The Yellow Six of the 1st Streetly Boy Scouts Troop achieved wide fame, at least in our road, at the top end, on the left hand side, for its unflagging efforts during World War II, collecting silver paper for recycling into Spitfires and Hurricanes. This enabled the Royal Air Force to sweep the Luftwaffe from the skies. The Yellow Six's tenacity finally drove Adolf Hitler to suicide and his generals to accept unconditional surrender (Churchill, Winston S: *The Second World War Vol 6*, p267, London 1954).

The attraction of the Boy Scouts as a movement, just before mid-century, was that it was vaguely military at a time when militarism was considered heroic - but it was military without one having to do beach landings under fire, or be parachuted behind enemy lines, or leopard crawl to Berlin. Even so, one did rugged things like go outside without a jersey. In fact we were ceaselessly encouraged, mainly by our parents, to get out of doors and stay out, and, once there, we were often able to do things that would have made our parents freak had they known - such as placing pennies on the railway line so that they were flattened into wide thin discs by passing locomotives; looking at pictures of Esther Williams and Jane Russell in bathing costumes; vaulting in unison over chasms and muddy creeks using our long Boy Scout poles, sometimes making it - in one go - to the other side. Sometimes not.

The Boy Scouts was undoubtedly a good institution for preparing boys for the cultural revolution which was about to burst upon the world. England was very prejudiced in these times, its population still being almost one hundred per cent white and protestant. But we were, inexorably, emerging from a period during which we considered ourselves a master race founded by men such as Biggles and now led by people such as Rockfist Rogan with clear instructions from God to show the world's backward nations (i.e. every country outside Europe but including Ireland) how to do just about everything.

Except cook, of course.

As black troops poured into Britain ready for the invasion of Europe in 1944 one was suddenly aware that blacks were normal people who did not, after all, eat each other. This was not only a revelation to us young boys, it was a great disappointment.

The Boy Scout High Command, with its great emphasis on world-wide links and brotherhood, was not blind to all this and even I, as humble L*E*A*D*E*R of the Peewit* Patrol (also known as the Yellow Six), saw it as my duty to prepare the Yellow Six for the advancing social revolution which was to end with Englishmen having to mix with people who were not only a different colour but who could hardly speak English.

This is why I introduced the Welsh Kid into our midst, despite the culture shock I knew it would bring. The move, as you will see, proved to be a good one and the lad rose to become accepted as almost our equal.

You might wonder, as you read some of the escapades in this book, if some of my colleagues in the Yellow Six were not, perhaps, well, let's put it this way... you might wonder if, in one or two cases, 'the lift was not going all the way to the top'. I often lay awake at night wondering this myself: were we *normal?*

The point to remember about those days in Britain is that the place was heavily polluted and it is, today, well documented how pollution and chemicals, leaching out of everyday objects, had serious effects on our head filler. For instance, the seemingly innocent aluminium pot is now suddenly under scrutiny because some neurologists believe aluminium contaminates food and may be a cause of that disease that destroys one's memory. I can't remember its name right now. When I was young, aluminium was the flavour of the era.

The peewit is the onomatopoeic name for the lapwing which was our patrol mascot. It is a black and white plover-like bird with a crest.

Author's Note

And mercury... In my boyhood we would play for hours with beads of mercury, breaking them up and watching them coalesce again. Today, mercury is known to scramble the brain just as surely as opening up the skull and inserting an electric eggbeater.

Warwickshire, where the Yellow Six did most of its inhaling, is home to some of Britain's heaviest industries and in the 1940s and 1950s smoke used to pour from stacks like toothpaste.

The Midlands' air was filled with sulphur dioxide, carbon monoxide, carbon dioxide, oxides of nitrogen, phenols, chlorofluorocarbons, lumps of soot and, for six years, German bombs. All brain damaging commodities.

And there was lead - lead from vehicle exhausts and from water pipes. Water, passing along lead pipes, becomes contaminated (hence the expression 'heavy water'). Of all common pollutants lead was the worst for damaging children's brains.

There was lead in the paint used for our cots, toys and walls and, according to medical people today, kids ingested lead by eating their cots, toys and walls although I have no recollection of doing this myself.

Most of the lead in our bodies was ingested via the fingers. For example, we played with lead soldiers and then ate sandwiches with lead-blackened fingers so the lead went into our stomachs from where - although I never understood how - it leaked upwards into our brains.

We even stripped the sheet lead trimmings from the fronts of bombed-out houses and melted it down on the kitchen stove so that our homes became filled with lead fumes. Whole families ended up sitting cross-eyed in corners, giggling and nudging each other until the authorities came and took them away.

I recall melting down some broken lead soldiers over the lounge fire, pouring the molten metal into a sand mould, and fashioning a model boat hull and trying to sail it in the bath. Any parent seeing their child engrossed in making a lead boat hull should immediately start asking it questions:

'Look at me son! Tell me, what day is it?'

'How many fingers am I holding up?'

As kids we might have been small, but we were *heavy*. Not surprisingly then, we were poor swimmers. Should we be foolish enough to dive into a pool our lead-filled heads acted like breeze blocks anchoring us to the bottom. Lifesavers, before knocking off at municipal swimming pools, would do a quick check around to see if there were any feet sticking up above the surface.

For this reason today's cheap plastic playthings may, after all, be an advantage over lead painted metal and wooden things. Certainly, plastic armbands are safer than lead ones.

In other words some of the actions of the Yellow Six should be seen in context with the above.

Hoping this finds you as it finds me.

James F Clarke

MAKING A BOB OR TWO

Bob-a-job, that annual Saturday event when Boy Scouts, the world over, used to offer their services around the community, is more or less a dead institution today. A pity because it was very character building.

We were prepared to do anything for a bob (a 'bob' was otherwise known as a shilling and worth in today's context five pence). We were even prepared to work. At the end of a hard bob-a-job day the Yellow Six, after much accounting, would end up with three or four bob. This was, of course, after deducting our subsistence and travel allowance.

When we came calling, villagers who knew us would barricade their doors or paint white crosses on them, but a few kind souls would go out of their way to find jobs for us such as turning three tons of compost or cleaning out the coal shed.

In 1946 the Yellow Six was booked a week in advance for bob-a-job by the Cowins who owned a chain of confectioners. By the time Saturday came we had worked ourselves into quite a froth of expectation, Laidlaw saying he was sure Mr Cowin would want us to wrap sweets or squirt jam into doughnuts. For this reason I suggested we all scrubbed our fingernails and made sure we smelled of Lifebuoy before we knocked at Cowin's door. We mustered outside the gate at 7am feeling unusually antiseptic and then marched up the drive in single file.

Making quite a display of our fingernails we saluted Mr Cowin. He asked us if we had brought our trek cart. Most troops had a large-wheeled trek cart in which they carried rope and tents and framed pictures of Jane Russell and the King. Thoughts filled our minds of being asked to take a trek cart full of sweets and sherbert sticks and distribute them, at our own discretion, among the underprivileged. But we had no cart. I said we would come up with a plan. Mr Cowin then asked us to follow him round the back. There we discovered Mr Cowin's second interest - keeping chickens.

He said he needed three sacks of chicken manure delivered to his brother near Four Oaks, five kilometres away. Hence the need for a trek cart. He would pay us ten bob, a sum of money which had us clutching at each other. We said we'd be back.

After some debate outside on the pavement we realised we were unlikely to find a cart and so decided to forget it and, instead, try our luck door-to-door.

We knocked on a door in Thornhill Road - a road of fairly large houses. At our very first house a distraught woman, who was new to the area, came to the door with a screaming baby which looked as if it had only recently been dropped by a stork. 'Bob-a-job!' I said, saluting. 'Can we be of service ma'am?' She grabbed me by my bird recognition badge 'Please!' she said, 'Take my other child for a walk in her pram!'

The infant was, I suppose, not much over one year. The pram was of high class coachwork like Buckingham Palace's Irish State Coach. It had high leaf springs and felt as if it had power steering. Everybody wanted first go. But, as L*E*A*D*E*R of the Yellow Six, I took first shift at pushing it. It was agreed, after a lot of unseemly shouting and shoving, that after 500 paces the others would get a turn in alphabetical order. Laidlaw then accused me of taking long steps. Arbuckle was next and we all said he was deliberately walking too fast for us to do an accurate count. In retaliation he started to run and the baby began to cry. We all stopped and peered under the canopy. We were assailed by the most nauseating stench. Even Laidlaw turned puce. The baby, on seeing us, stopped crying and smiled.

Arbuckle suddenly announced he had completed his 500 steps. I said I had counted only 250. The Welsh Kid said 100. We all said yes, 100. Then the Welsh Kid, who was never a slow thinker, shouted 'Chicken

Making a Bob or Two

manure!' or something synonymous. We looked at him. Bongo! With the pram we could easily move three bags of manure in one haul.

To cut a long story short we raced back to the Cowins', dumped the three bags on the pram (remembering to move the baby to the far end) and roared off to Four Oaks taking shifts of twenty paces each which was as long as any of us could hold our breath. It began to rain. The pram, the whole soggy pile, was now releasing enough nitrogen, methane and other greenhouse gases to turn Britain into a tropical wonderland. It also seemed to anaesthetise the child who grinned continuously in a cross-eyed sort of way.

We delivered the goods and, somewhat overdue, raced back to Thornhill Road. The distraught mother, supported by neighbours and a totally sympathetic Constable Cope (who, for some reason, kept all our names in his notebook), rushed to the pram and took out her baby.

As she blissfully hugged the noisome little bundle of mostly you-know-what, burying her lips time and time again in the soiled chicken feathers adhering to it, I thought to myself what a wonderful thing was mother love.

She never did pay us.

WARTIME AND SEX PROBLEMS

Perhaps I should begin at the beginning.

I was (to use that unfortunate expression) 'brought up' in London but, as soon as the Germans began their timeous campaign to create much needed public open space in our particularly crowded borough, the Clarke family was transferred to the quiet little village of Streetly some twenty kilometres north of Birmingham. My father, who was involved in the early days of plastics manufacturing, was not called up during World War II because his work was considered of strategic importance. He left London to work in a small factory half-concealed on the edge of a pretty silver birch woodland on Streetly's western border. I am not sure to this day what he was doing, but I do know that he spoke of it only out of the corner of his mouth. He also did his bit for Britain by joining the ARP, a voluntary corps whose members ran around during and after air raids tidying up after the Germans. ARP stood for Air Raid Precautions though my mother insisted it stood for ''anging Round Pubs'.

We knew suffering of course. For the six years of war we were forced to eat our crusts. And we would queue from dawn at Gillings the grocer's when a shipment of oranges came in from South Africa - and come away with one for each child in the family and purple stamps in our ration books. Clothes and shoes were also rationed and the shoes we wore were made of compressed cardboard. My mother hammered into the soles stout metal studs called Segs. Even my sister, who cried piteously about the indignity of it, had to wear Segs. The idea was to save our soles because there was a wartime shortage of cows and, therefore, of leather.

When my sister and I walked down Foley Road we sounded like the Brigade of Guards. Dull red sparks flew from our shoes in all directions, sometimes setting fire to hayfields.

Walking on Segs was like wearing roller skates because they elevated one some distance above the ground. For years I never knew what it was to walk at ground level and it was only in 1945, when the war ended and the cows came home, and we could walk around without Segs, that I discovered I was quite a short fellow.

A couple of years after the war our biology mistress announced that the time had come to teach us about animal reproduction. We could all sense that she was hugely embarrassed because in those days sex was like Operation Overlord, the plan to invade Europe - one simply never talked about it. We were appallingly ignorant about it because, after all, there were no late night TV films with men springing into bed with women and, in books, when the man took the woman in his arms and her robe slipped off her shoulders to the floor, the author would resort to using dots into infinity... We were so marvellously ignorant about where babies came from that most kids happily accepted the stork theory. Those of us who were more scientifically informed subscribed to the cabbage patch theory.

Wartime and Sex Problems

Our teacher, looking at the floor, asked if any of us knew anything about sex. I thought she had said 'Segs' and that she wanted to reminisce about the war, so my hand shot up. She was surprised - I think everybody was - but she bade me say my piece and I began saying how if you had lots of Segs it made you walk tall and how really good Segs could set hayfields on fire. I told her how it took me quite a long time to get used to Segs and how, quite often, I would end up on my back.

Noticing the way her eyes snapped open I warmed to the subject and told her how, the more Segs you had, the longer your shoe leather lasted. And I said how, thank goodness, Segs down at the village cost very little and how the cobbler's wife would even give a discount.

At this stage she held up her hand for silence and bade us turn to page 117 of our textbooks and read, quietly to ourselves, about sexual reproduction in the common newt.

THE GREAT ESCAPE

My father, as an air raid warden, was very active. The fact that the Germans never managed to drop a bomb on him attests to this. He would frequently pop out in the evening to look for chinks of light that might be showing from houses whose black-out curtains were not properly closed. Air raid wardens wore black uniforms and black steel helmets so that enemy bomb-aimers would have difficulty spotting them. If bombs dropped, the wardens would rush up with stirrup pumps which were worked by hand and which squirted water. We were endlessly fascinated by an item in the ARP's written orders regarding stirrup pumps. It read 'In the event of water not being available, improvise.'

The ARP's local nerve centre was a heavily sandbagged former shop on the Chester Road, a kilometre from our house. It was said to have had a secret underground pipeline to the nearby Hardwick Arms public bar. It also had a billiard table, dartboard, library of lascivious paperbacks, an enormous bar and pictures on the walls of ladies who had obviously run out of clothing coupons. When my father went out looking for chinks this was usually as far as he got.

If, perchance, my father was at home asleep when the air raid sirens sounded - and they sounded fairly frequently because the Germans, when bombing Birmingham, would often retreat over Streetly and shake out any loose bombs they had left over - he would shout terrible threats to the enemy before beginning to don his woolly combinations, his shirt and tie (he always wore a tie, even when looking for chinks), his black trousers and battle blouse, and then his thick black greatcoat, army boots and gaiters. Then he would place upon his head his black and shining helmet with W (warden) stencilled in white. This was an extremely heavy item and my father said it was to protect him from falling bombs. My older sister, Ann, observed that if a bomb ever did fall on his head he would have the devil's own job getting his helmet off.

My father would complete his ensemble by tying a police whistle round his neck and slinging the stirrup pump over his shoulder. By the time he had finished dressing the 'all clear' might have sounded and he would begin, slowly, to reverse the procedure, stopping every now and again to shake his fist at the retreating enemy. Sometimes there was a second wave of bombers and he would have to start all over again.

Despite his daytime job making secret plastic things with which to confound the Third Reich, and his duties as a warden at night, my father still found time to make all the important decisions around our house. While my mother decided how to make the food ration spin out and how to clothe us and keep us supplied with books and how we were to get to school ten kilometres away, it was my father who, poring over maps of Nazi-occupied Europe, would be deciding whether it was time for the Allies to open up a second front and what Churchill should tell Roosevelt.

My mother also took the war very seriously and the first thing she did when war broke out was to have a baby. On September 7, four days after Britain declared war on Germany, my younger sister was born. My mother named her Victoria because, she said, it would make Britain victorious. It was uncanny how she was always right.

Within days of this event she began digging up our entire garden - about half an acre - lawns, flower beds, the lot. She then planted potatoes, cabbage, cauliflower, sprouts and beans in response to the Government's appeal for the British public to 'Dig for Victory'. She won prizes and certificates, and wolf whistles as convoys of troops rumbled past on manoeuvres and saw her digging furiously for victory. We became self-supporting in vegetables and fed some of our neighbours too. Britain, until then an importer of half its food needs, now became self-sufficient.

My father decided our family should become self-supporting in meat too and one day came home with a pair of rabbits. We kept them in a hutch where they begat with biblical enthusiasm and we gave each new arrival a name. This is fatal, of course, because you then have to decide whether to eat Jerome or Prunella, Bunbuns or Big Ears. We found we could not kill any of them and eventually the bunnies, like prisoners of war which, of course, they were, escaped under the wire one moonless night, ate all the cabbages, and fanned out through the countryside never to be seen again.

HOW A DOG CAN TEACH LEADERSHIP

One of the characteristics of the British people and their singular relationship with animals was that, in those days, most people kept dogs as pets and not as a means of deterring burglars. Nowadays, an Englishman keeps a dog - usually a big dog with the dental battery of a *Tyrannosaurus-rex* - only because he cannot afford a bazooka.

About the time I joined the Scouts, it was decided I needed a dog because it would be character building. A small dog was 'out' and you wouldn't dare buy a dachshund during the war. People would actually hiss at dachshunds because they were associated with Germany which is why, even to this day, dachshunds in England look at you out of the corners of their eyes. A big dog was appropriate, said mother, because I could then 'command' it to do things, thus improving my leadership abilities.

We went to buy the dog from a large woman who bred military guard dogs of up to seventeen hands - dogs trained to snap the kneecaps off people found creeping around secret installations at night. I cannot recall the breed, but its head and shoulders were quite a distance above sea level and its skin seemed to be sliding off its forehead and over its eyes in deep troubled folds. You could still see its eyes though. They were inclined to roll about showing lots of white like our biology teacher contemplating the delights of Segs. I asked what the dog ate and the woman said it had been brought up on pig offal. I was going to say I was not surprised it had brought up but my mother, sensing this, silenced me with a look. The woman added, through narrowed eyes, that it was also fond of children.

I dragged Mugger home (I named it after the giant Australian man-eating crocodile) and he immediately irrigated the front room carpet. My mother, instead of admonishing the dog, admonished me. She said that I must 'take command' and get it outside. I said 'Come Mugger', but the dog, which appeared to have a five litre bladder, rolled its eyes and made another puddle. Then my mother said 'Out!' and out it went.

'You see,' she said, 'be assertive.'

In the garden Mugger bounded all over the place wetting everything that stood upright including my leg. I knew enough about animals to know that when an animal widdled against your person it was openly challenging your authority and, unless you acted immediately, it would hunt you down for ever more every time it needed something against which to cock its leg. So I exercised some leadership and kicked it. It then, without looking up, widdled against my other leg.

While I taught Mugger nothing at all, it taught me to turn round and round each time I sat down and to chase people on bicycles.

One day it ate my new cricket ball and I lost my temper and called it every name that came to mind. I cranked out my entire repertoire of filth. It was as if a municipal sewer pipe had burst inside my mind. Neighbours called their children inside and shut the windows. Mother came out, pulled me into the house by my ear, and washed my mouth out with carbolic soap. The dog, which had ambled in after us, now lay, head on paws, watching the froth dribble down my chin. It rolled its eyes.

Eventually the dog and I became good friends and I owed it a great deal for its guidance which doubtless gave me what was needed to eventually lead the Yellow Six in its stand against the German war machine.

How a Dog Can Teach Leadership

THE YELLOW SIX - THE CAST

I must introduce you to the individuals who made up the Yellow Six:
   Laidlaw, Vincent: deputy leader of the Yellow Six. Laidlaw was the tallest and oldest of us. He was the son of a high-ranking police officer and always carried a bayonet lashed to his staff. He was good at languages and was known for his grim adherence to the Boy Scout rule: 'A Scout smiles and whistles under all difficulties.' He frequently got us into difficulties, but always with a smile. In later life he became a famous sub-accountant in a Middlesbrough building society.
   Bodley-Smith, Julian: son of a Walsall leather manufacturer. He was the only one in our patrol who did not wear Segs. Quiet and intrepid. He had an intolerable sister named Felicity who, like one or two other females one meets, was handicapped by a high intelligence. She was a frequent irritant. Like his father, Julian Bodley-Smith now makes things out of cows.

The Yellow Six - The Cast

Watson, Graham: father was an RAF fighter pilot who smoked a pipe and who never spoke of his exploits, even though, as a Spitfire pilot, he fought in the Battle of Britain. As L*E*A*D*E*R of the Yellow Six I tried to model my own character on Watson Snr. Watson was always incredibly clean. He became a diplomat in West Africa.

Arbuckle, Egbert: had large feet which were very useful when walking in swamps. He was astonishingly resourceful and, in neurotic pursuance of the Boy Scout motto 'be prepared', carried a wondrous variety of things in his bulging pockets including spanners, quick-drying cement, a pebble for sucking, etc, etc. He was, in effect, one enormous survival kit. Became a professional footballer and in later life coached soccer at a Manchester girls' school.

The Welsh Kid: real name forgotten except it mostly comprised L's. Very small but alert as a fox terrier. Was probably first alien accepted into the Boy Scout movement in England. Was always treated as an equal despite funny accent. Used in many of our experiments. Returned, voluntarily, to Aberystwyth where he became a schoolmaster.

Clarke, James F: the L*E*A*D*E*R of the Yellow Six. Again, I stress, I am saying this as one of the most modest of the 20th Century's movers and shakers. Headed campaign to collect silver paper for The War Effort (Strang, Sir Keith: *The Role of Streetly Boy Scouts in the Supply of Materials in World War II*, London 1968; Werkmeister, Field Marshall Werner: *Silver Paper and the Downfall of the Third Reich*, Munich 1970).

I should also explain how it was we acquired the Welsh Kid.

One had to swear, as a Boy Scout, never to differentiate between 'colour, creed or class' and, as L*E*A*D*E*R of the Yellow Six, I was deeply aware of this code and felt it necessary to demonstrate, to the world, my own patrol's high level of social tolerance. As soon as I mentioned to the lads that I was allowing a Welsh kid to join us, Bodley-Smith wanted to know if he was Catholic. 'Of course not!' I said. Was he coloured? I was again able to reassure Bodley-Smith. For a start his skin was a sort of pink, his hair red, his eyes green - how could he be coloured?

He already had his firelighter's badge for having demonstrated he could light a camp fire with only two cigarette lighters (in Wales, where it never stops raining, the rules allow this). In truth, we needed the Welsh Kid because his fiery Welsh temperament could help us fight off the blue patrol (the Gannets) and the red patrol (the Bulls). This may sound like colour prejudice to some, but it had nothing to do with skin colour. It was just the little coloured flashes which each patrol wore on its shirt fronts that ignited our passions.

I also favoured the Welsh Kid because he said he came from 'Wells' instead of Wales and when he talked about going home he would say 'goo-inn hoom' and this, I knew, would keep the lads amused. As a measure of my judgement of character, let it be once more noted that the Welsh Kid rose to become accepted almost on a level with an Englishman.

YELLOW SIX TO THE RESCUE

The war was a good time to be a Scout because, apart from helping with The War Effort (which included collecting waste with which to hit the Germans) there was also such a shortage of manpower that it meant Boy Scouts were often called upon when a lot of hands were needed.

One grey November afternoon I heard, over the radio, that the police were seeking volunteers to search Sutton Park for a missing woman. We marched to the police station and, as most of us wore Segs, we made quite an imperialistic noise. As we swung into the Police Station everybody looked up including Chief Inspector Victor Rex Cogbill who had been seconded to co-ordinate the hunt. It was, of course, a Boy Scout's duty to 'serve God and the King' and we instinctively recognised that Inspector Victor Rex Cogbill represented both.

But there was a distinct raising of the eyes when Streetly's Constable Cope saw us. He towered above us, which was not difficult, and knew us collectively and individually. He suggested to the Inspector that it would not be wise to have Boy Scouts wandering around the moors, especially as it was near dusk, and especially as the missing woman might have been murdered.

Murdered!

Now we were really keen. We all began tugging at the Inspector's sleeve. He then nodded to the Constable who, with undisguised reluctance, allocated us a sector of the park which was particularly soggy. We carried our patrol whistle which had a pea in it and we were told to blow it loudly if we saw or found anything.

We walked through strings of cold mist, down into the dale, singing patriotic songs in deep voices in the hope that if the murderer was in there somewhere he would think the Eighth Army was bearing down upon him. Although the sun was still two hours from setting, the afternoon was gloomy and foreboding. Soon we were shivering and up to our ankles in black ooze.

Our voices trailed off and we lapsed into a silence. It was then we became aware of the distant baying of bloodhounds and our hair stood on end despite the weight of Brylcreem.

As it grew dark we closed up.

Each of us carried a scout staff, a long pole made from ash which Boy Scouts use for vaulting streams and building arch bridges similar to the Sydney Harbour Bridge. None of us had really mastered the art even of vaulting streams but we never gave up trying. As we advanced into the swamp I let Vincent Laidlaw go in front because, well, first it was good to give everybody a go at leading, and second, he had a bayonet lashed to his staff.

Darkness fell. We were frequently sinking up to our knees in mud and were keeping so close together we kept standing on each other's feet - except Arbuckle whose enormous feet enabled him to walk on the surface.

Somebody said 'What if we run into the murderer?' Nobody answered the question but we closed up even tighter. It now became impossible to move in any direction, especially as we all had our eyes tightly shut. I decided to blow on the whistle but the pea kept popping out.

Late that night a huge spotlight that should have attracted enemy bombers from as far away as Schleswig Holstein began sweeping the marsh and it finally settled on us. There were dogs and voices and, in the white glare, some agitated mother-looking figures. A loudhailer said 'Walk this way!' We then learned that the hunt for the missing woman had been called off hours ago and that she had not been missing after all, but had merely been at the cinema. In those days you could sit at the pictures all day for a shilling.

The police had spent the evening looking for us. There stood Constable Cope. This time he made no pretence at hiding it: his eyes were definitely raised right up into his forehead so that they looked like a pair of picnic eggs.

THE SECRET ROLE OF THE SILVER BALL

Recycling is, today, a sort of 'green' religious tenet. But few people appreciate the glorious history of recycling and the role it played during World War II when the Government appealed for every spare saucepan, every railing and iron gate and every scrap of foil for turning into aeroplanes and even battleships and tanks. The Yellow Six won the area prize for collecting the most silver paper for turning into fighter planes.

Our persistence in collecting silver paper was an important contributing factor towards Britain's defeat of the Germans in the air. Everybody said so. Yet all that was ever said, officially, of our feat - although the Yellow Six as such was not specifically named - was when Winston Churchill said, 'Never in the field of human conflict was so much owed by so many to so few.'

We used to scavenge the silver paper from chocolate wrappers and cigarette packets and make a big ball out of it. The whole thing was so sticky it held wonderfully together and smelled delightfully of a mixture of mature Player's Virginia Leaf and Cadbury's and Fry's chocolate.

At about the time our very first ball of silver paper grew to football size, and we began parading it around the village, German bombers hit Streetly for the first time. This puzzled the village elders. What could the Germans be aiming at? True, Streetly was on the route which fleeing German bombers took after bombing Birmingham (and they'd dump any unused bombs) but this first raid seemed to be a concerted attack with bombs falling among the houses and not just in

The Yellow Six

The Secret Role of the Silver Ball

the fields. The Germans couldn't possibly be after the one and only factory. It was, after all, hidden in a wood and nobody even spoke of it except in whispers and many of us even looked the other way when we went past.

To me it was obvious: the Germans had decided the quickest way to end the RAF's superiority in the air would be to hit at its vital sources of raw materials and it was now obvious they had got wind of our latest silver ball. They were determined to get it before it got them.

We decided to stop parading it around the village or even referring to it except in indirect terms. We developed a way of soliciting for silver paper with lowered voices speaking behind our hands. Everybody understood. But the Germans dropped more bombs. My mother said it was probably the starlight reflecting off the silver ball that gave them a reference point. Stoically we continued to collect (we owed it to Britain), but now we hid the ball under sacks.

Then one day the air raid sirens went during school time. Now, our school was ten kilometres from Streetly and far from any strategic target worthy of a risky daylight bombing raid. In a heady mixture of excitement and fear we filed into the tunnel leading down to half a dozen subterranean air raid shelters where Miss Blanesworth led us in singing 'Run Rabbit, Run' and 'It's a Long Way to Tipperary' and other deeply patriotic songs. Voices began wavering as we heard bombs getting nearer and nearer and Miss Blanesworth was now hitting notes shrill enough to microwave an Aberdeen Angus.

Only I knew what it was all about - the Germans, having failed to get The Ball, were now out to get our school and so rub out the Yellow Six.

As it happened the bombs were all a hoax. The crump! crump! CRUMP! was Vincent Laidlaw deliberately banging the heavy door at the entrance to the air raid shelter tunnel, louder and louder. He had a fine sense of the dramatic, did my deputy.

The Germans, despite repeated attempts over the years, never did hit our ball and eventually Hitler called the *Luftwaffe* off. Then an RAF officer came to our village to collect our latest ball and he gave the Yellow Six the highest honour bestowed upon young people who defied the German might - a Certificate.

The Secret Role of the Silver Ball

THE SHELTER THE GERMANS NEVER FOUND

Towards the end of the war many people in Britain gave up using their air raid shelters. This was because the Germans had run out of bombers following the depredations by chocolate and virginia leaf flavoured Spitfires. Throughout Britain, the corrugated iron shelters were beginning to fill up with garden tools, broken furniture and assorted junk. The one in our garden became the secret headquarters of the Yellow Six and from it we plotted the final downfall of Adolf Hitler whom or who (or whatever) we eventually drove to suicide and whose generals we drove to ignominious surrender (Warner, P: *The Secret Forces of World War II*, London 1985).

From the very beginning of the war, our Anderson shelter was, at my mother's insistence, sunk into a pit in the garden and covered by an elaborate rockery. This was so the Germans would not spot us as they passed 20,000 feet overhead. Her precautions paid off. I doubt the Germans ever suspected that our family had a shelter.

We were often slow in getting down to the shelter, especially on those clear, freezing nights when, if an arm so much as slipped from under the bed covers, it would quickly turn black and have to be amputated. In any event my sisters always had to rush back for some favourite doll and I, too, was tardy, sometimes finding it difficult to dig my way out from under the blankets and work out where the bedroom door was. One night, just as we all piled into the shelter and got the candle lit, my mother announced she must go back for her teeth. 'For goodness sake, woman,' said my father, 'they're dropping bombs not frankfurters.'

The Shelter the Germans Never Found

The truth is we liked the excitement of the shelter and of being allowed to peep out at the sky red with the fires from the air raid. During the war, although we spent our time in rural Warwickshire and Staffordshire where the spacing between bombs was quite generous compared with London, we occasionally went up to London where we stayed with an aunt on Mitcham Common. There I saw, for the first time, an indoor Morrison shelter - a stout iron frame which supported a bed. When wakened by air raid sirens you simply rolled off the bed and under it. Nobody, to my knowledge, ever used these shelters, at least not if they slept upstairs, which most Londoners did, because there was the prospect of dropping through the floor if a bomb dismantled the house. Instead, everybody would open the windows and lean out and ooh and aah as the searchlights picked up enemy bombers and as the ack ack shells exploded into little puffs of smoke in the sky.

When in London, I preferred to go down into public shelters and see the wondrous array of night attire and the courting couples who had been caught out coming home in the dark, as well as the fascinating posters saying 'Careless talk costs lives' and one which read:

IF AN INCENDIARY BOMB FALLS, DO NOT LOSE YOUR HEAD - PUT IT IN A BUCKET AND PLACE SAND ON TOP.

THE POWER OF OBSERVATION

Another type of shelter that fascinated us was found along many streets and was simply a brick-built box for ducking into should a high explosive bomb or, towards the end of the war, a 'doodlebug' (self-propelled bomb) or V2 rocket, come crashing down. You had to be very observant.

Our scoutmaster, Thistlethwaite, used to say that by observing you not only avoided direct hits from bombs but you also fed the brain. The more observations you stuffed into your brain box the larger it would grow until, like the stomach, it would permanently expand. You could end up with a fat head like Einstein. Thistlethwaite had a thing about constantly looking up and behind oneself and he was fond of quoting from *Scouting for Boys* the words of Lord Baden-Powell:

A scout must not only look to his front, but also to either side and behind ... often, by suddenly looking back, you will see an enemy's scout or a thief showing himself.

'Often' showing himself?

Thistlethwaite would then cry out 'Ob-ser-VATION!' and make us all jump. He sent us out on observation patrol through Sutton Park, which began quite near the Scout Hall. We had to report back in an hour. Carrying our stream-vaulting poles at the trail, we walked single file because one cannot see much walking in a gaggle. In a gaggle you could all fall into a bog whereas in single file only the front fellow would fall in and the rest could then use him as a stepping stone.

The Power of Observation

The act of looking sideways and backwards while walking in single file made progress rather ragged. There was much shunting when somebody suddenly stopped because he fancied he had spotted 'an enemy scout or thief showing himself'.

I should explain that the Yellow Six, like all Boy Scout patrols, had its own unique animal symbol. We were in fact the Peewit patrol and our secret signal was the call of the peewit (or lapwing), a crested bird which went 'peee-witt!' By calling 'peewit' we could keep in touch without the enemy realising that it was us making the racket. Had the Germans ever invaded Britain we could have so confused them with our secret calls they would have ended up milling around back on the landing beaches. We were told about scouts in other patrols who could make such authentic sounds that their designated birds and other animals followed them around and even sat on their shoulders in quite large numbers. But not us. If the truth be told, none of us had ever seen or heard a peewit and this led the Welsh Kid to observe that it would make more sense if we all mooed like cattle. Sometimes we did both.

The Power of Observation

We came to a deep, dark birchwood. The Welsh Kid took the lead. (As L*E*A*D*E*R I would decide who would lead and, as I have already stated, I believed in giving everybody a chance, especially in dark woods or swamps.) We stopped peewitting and mooing and crept forward, looking mostly over our shoulders for thieves showing themselves. Thus we began running into trees and sometimes all six of us were silently concertinaed up against a single tree.

It was in the wood that we made our Observation.

It involved the Welsh Kid's older sister, Bronwyn. Now Bronwyn, who must have been eighteen or so, had flowing red hair and two beautiful legs (oh, how many times I counted them) and I lived in awe of her. Whenever she so much as acknowledged my presence I was struck dumb. Even if I managed to open my mouth nothing would come out, except dribble, and sometimes I could not get it closed except under medical supervision.

Patently Bronwyn was oblivious to our presence. She was leaning against a tree looking up with her great saucer eyes at a tall American sergeant. Now an American soldier was every boy's hero, not so much because of their nippy Jeeps and big silver Super Fortresses but because they sometimes could be induced to hand out chewing gum. At this stage most of the Yellow Six still preferred gum to girls.

We all ducked down in the undergrowth and watched, entranced, as the giggling Bronwyn began to unbutton her blouse. The soldier, meanwhile, was looking sideways and backwards - thus he spotted us. He came at us like the Santa Fe Express and we fled through bog and heather, vaulting wide streams with our poles in perfect unison, and eventually vaulted the park fence itself and stampeded into the Scout Hall, muddied, bloodied and fighting for breath.

What did you observe?' asked the startled Thistlethwaite.

'Nothing!' we said.

The Yellow Six

THE LAST ELEPHANTS IN ENGLAND

Some may wonder how it was that I led the Yellow Six when it is only in the Wolf Cubs that groups of six are generally formed. Indeed, a group of cubs is led by a 'sixer'. Our group of six Boy Scouts - and we were indeed real Boy Scouts with pointy hats and incredibly dangerous knives - was a complete patrol despite its low number. We remained only six because, well, nobody else would join us. I suppose the flies bothered them.

The 'yellow' label had to do with the yellow tabs we wore on our shirts. As I have explained (please find), each Scout patrol had an animal as a mascot and each animal was identified by a different colour tab.

A green and black tab meant the Scouts were of the Eagle patrol whose members aspired to 'soar like an eagle'. This was a very casualty-prone patrol. The Beaver patrol resolved to 'work hard' and wore blue and yellow; the Wolf patrol, with its yellow and black, was 'true unto death'. There was a Hippo patrol but I was never sure what they aspired to do - presumably float around in swamps.

As each patrol crept about in the park, members would keep in touch by making noises appropriate to their chosen animal. The Wolf patrol howled and the Bulldog patrol barked; the Elephant patrol trumpeted while the Bat patrol went (according to Baden-Powell's instructions) 'Pitz-pitz'. This was to mask one's presence by fooling picnickers into assuming there were merely wolves passing through the park, or a small herd of elephants, or a flock of eagles, and people would carry on, oblivious, playing ball or picking ants out of their sandwiches.

My patrol was originally the Jaguar patrol which had yellow flashes. In *Scouting for Boys* the jaguar call is described as: 'tongue in side of mouth - Keeook!' We soon found that creeping around the park crying 'Keeook!' attracted unwanted attention and picnickers would sometimes call a park attendant or pack up their kids and go home. The Elephant patrol had bigger problems. So did the Gannets so far from the sea, with their cry of 'Aaarrr'. The Hyena patrol, which had to emit 'a laughing cry - Ooowah-oowah-wah', were sometimes set upon by whole families. After all, the last hyena to be seen in the English Midlands was in the late Pleistocene and older people obviously had unhappy memories of them.

Anyway, our jaguar cry of 'Keeook' didn't sound very fierce so we changed to an animal whose sound was at least easy to mimic - the peewit. This call startled but never frightened picnickers.

Our change from being the Jaguar patrol to the Peewit patrol was not the first time we had changed animal mascots. Originally we were the Woodpecker patrol whose official call was 'heear flearfle' which, we discovered, the British public was not yet ready for. The peewit's colour tab was green and white. But as our mothers had already changed our tabs from woodpecker (red and white) to jaguar (yellow) they steadfastly refused to change tabs for a third time. So the peewits retained the yellow jaguar tabs - and hence the 'yellow' in the illustrious Yellow Six.

The Last Elephants in England

TRAILING BEHIND FELICITY

We were, in our own estimation, pretty good backwoodsmen. We could, for instance, track a herd of cows with ease. But one earned one's tracker's proficiency badge by actually tracking a person and in our case it had to be done across the wilds of Sutton Park. You followed the person by noticing subtle clues he left behind, such as toffee papers, felled trees, clumps of knotted grass whose heads would point in the direction you must take, and the occasional enigmatic sign scratched on the ground reading THIS WAY.

The Yellow Six decided to pass its tracker's test as a unit. We chose a glorious Sunday morning when the rain was relatively warm.

We were, to say the least, dismayed when Bodley-Smith turned up with his kid sister, aged about nine. He explained that his parents had gone to Birmingham, leaving him to babysit.

Felicity Bodley-Smith was very bright, but she had more serious faults than that. She came dressed in a white frilly dress like Shirley Temple and was wearing white patent leather shoes. Her conspicuousness made a mockery of our camouflage. It became pointless for us to creep around disguising our presence and communicating, as we usually did, with clever mimicry of the peewit. We stood out a mile with this Christmas fairy in our midst.

So, with our poles at the slope, we marched to the Big Oak from where Thistlethwaite said he would start the trail. He had risen early that morning, laid the trail and then, presumably, gone back to bed. We searched in vain for the first directional sign while Felicity skipped

Trailing Behind Felicity

around picking daisies. Eventually she asked us what we were looking for. She then indicated a clump of tall grass tied in a knot and pointing towards some woods.

We all agreed we would have spotted it by ourselves had we really been trying.

We came to a fork in the path and I motioned the patrol to stand back for fear they might obliterate any signs - a pebble placed upon a large stone for example would mean 'this is the right way' and a pebble placed in front of a larger one would mean 'take this new direction'. We searched in vain until, just before I was about to spot them, Felicity pointed to fresh blaze marks on trees.

We followed the marks through the woods and out on to open heath where I soon spotted a sign and turned left. Then right. Then left.

Using our poles we vaulted a muddy creek but came short. Felicity found stepping stones. We pole-vaulted a second creek and landed, as a well-synchronised team, ankle deep in black mud. Then we hit a firm trail along which, as I pointed out to my patrol, many people had recently passed. I was able to show them how these footprints were recent and were probably made by dozens of people, one with very large feet like Arbuckle.

Felicity said, in her armour-piercing voice, that these were our footprints. We had, she said, gone in a circle.

'What do we do now?' I said before I could stop myself. This phrase, of course, is the last phrase that should escape a leader's lips. Felicity said she would show us where we went wrong and she skipped ahead pointing out little arrows scratched in the ground, and stones placed upon stones and knotted grass and blazed trees. I had to tell her to get behind us because, after all, who was leading this patrol? She or I? Or she or me? Or all three of us?

We eventually found the end of the trail near the Sutton Coldfield gate deep in a holly thicket. There was an envelope tacked to a tree and a message inside reading 'Well done the Peewits!' Muddied and bedraggled though we were we glowed with triumph.

What detracted from it all was the sight of Felicity's white patent leather shoes - they were spotless, like her stupid dress.

THE ART OF SMILING WHILE WHISTLING

In days like these, what with the stress created by who gets to operate the remote control and the incessant fear of being caught with nothing to give muggers, one of the most useful rules for everyday survival is the Scout rule: 'A Scout smiles and whistles under all difficulties.' This is not easy. For a start you cannot smile and whistle at the same time. You have to smile, then whistle, smile, then whistle, smile, then whistle...

When I was L*E*A*D*E*R of the Yellow Six we were helping a workman who had fallen from some scaffolding to sort out his legs from the metal poles that had descended with him. The man was heavy and not really co-operative on account (it later transpired) of a compound fracture of the tibia which, now that I come to look back, I think we must have kept treading on.

Our scoutmaster, Thistlethwaite, had only just told us about the smiling-and-whistling-under-all-difficulties bit and now, here we were, presented with a God-given difficulty - a bad-tempered, injured person entangled with heavy scaffolding. Vincent Laidlaw, the strongest of us, pulled away the iron poles while whistling 'Put another nickel in, in the nickelodeon'. We joined spiritedly in the chorus. The injured man eventually shouted to us to shut up. We decided to have one more chorus before abandoning him.

Laidlaw said he would never have lived anyway.

As I say, smiling and whistling under all difficulties is not always easy. Just try it, for instance, when under heavy cross examination for knocking down a policeman above the rank of constable or when being

The Art of Smiling While Whistling

held up by an unfriendly robber, or falling off the stern of a liner around 120°W 39°S.

The entire 1st Streetly Boy Scouts was discussing such issues round the camp fire one weekend when somebody mentioned the stoicism shown by Red Indian braves. With meat hooks through their stomach walls they were hoisted over a fire. They were not supposed to wince even. I suppose the eyes were allowed to smart a bit. Thistlethwaite was dead against us trying this out on the Welsh Kid, who was the nearest thing we knew to a Red Indian and whom we all admired for the minimum amount of snivelling he did when he cut himself on his 4.5 kg multi-purpose scout knife.

Thistlethwaite, to take our minds off meat hooks, opened up *Scouting for Boys* and read to us about scouts in other parts of the world. Before he knew what he was reading, he was recounting Baden-Powell's yarn about Yaghan scouts in Patagonia who drive spears into their own thighs 'and smile all the time'. Thistlethwaite wouldn't let us drive our sheath knives into our own thighs, or even the Welsh Kid's thigh, or even shove burning brands into each other's ear holes.

In the end we had to be content with shooting elastic bands at each other.

TWENTY-FOUR GOOD DEEDS IN ONE TINY COIN

The Boy Scout's Promise, to do a good deed every day, is a very solemn one and comes from the knights of old who would ride up and down the countryside dressed in mild steel looking for opportunities to do good deeds such as giving to the poor or fighting dragons. Doing a good deed a day has a great impact on one's character in later life and a scout, in order to remember to do his daily good deed, is supposed to tie a knot in his handkerchief. If, at the end of the day, he has not done a good deed he has to do two the next day.

Except for Watson, we never carried handkerchiefs. Only sissies and wets and, sometimes, grammar school boys, carried hankies. We used our sleeves.

For this reason we tended to forget to do our good deeds and one day Vincent Laidlaw and I found ourselves summoned to appear before Thistlethwaite. He was cross. He had emerged from the Scout Hall shouting for us to drop whatever we were doing and report to him. It was unfortunate that, at that precise moment, we were practising how to rescue victims who were leaping from burning buildings. By working as a team, one can catch lots of people jumping out of windows. Six of you simply run up and down the pavement holding a blanket pulled really taut - like a trampoline. But it needed practice. Indeed, by suddenly pulling the blanket extra taut just as the plummeting victim makes contact with it, you can bounce him straight back up.

Twenty-four Good Deeds in One Tiny Coin

Assuming there are no more victims to rescue, you can sharpen your skills by keeping the last jumpee airborne for ages.

A poorly built scout named Bird - appropriately enough - had volunteered to climb to the top of the Scout Hall to play the part of the victim, and was, in fact, already on his way down and approaching terminal velocity when Thistlethwaite demanded we drop everything. In retrospect it was silly of us to have let go right then but one thinks of such things only afterwards when one sees the paramedics setting up their drips.

We reported to Thistlethwaite, clicking the heels and saluting until, slightly exasperated, he told us to stop. He wanted to tell us that when it came to doing good deeds we were ten days in arrears, and he reminded us that we were L*E*A*D*E*R and deputy-leader of the Peewit patrol and should be setting an example.

He challenged us to make up the arrears during the course of that very day. Laidlaw and I liked nothing more than a good challenge and we clicked the heels and saluted before striding purposefully towards the village looking for little old ladies to help across the road or on to buses. With the really very old and very doddery we found any bus would do.

The Boy Scout manual says that removing a stone from a horse's hoof is a typical good deed. In fact a scout knife has, among its many blades, a large spike just for this sort of thing. It can also be used for hurrying old folk across the road or to help them leap aboard buses. But horses, even in those days, were becoming scarce and those that still pulled carts or galloped along with people bouncing up and down on their backs, never seemed to get stones in their hooves.

A more typical good deed was 'to drop a coin in a poor man's cap'. In those days a single penny was enough to buy you a slab of chocolate from the railway station slot machine. For this reason alone I found it difficult to drop pennies into poor men's hats and certainly never felt the 'after glow' that Thistlethwaite spoke about. Mostly I felt sick afterwards. Once, when I rashly put a penny in a beggar's hat I returned next day and took it back.

As we patrolled the village, looking about us all the time in search of good deeds and making everybody nervous, Laidlaw hit on the idea of 'buying ourselves' out of trouble.

He showed me a sixpence. 'Here,' he said, 'are twenty-four good deeds in the palm of my hand.'

Now in those days, we still had farthings. There were four farthings in a penny and twelve pennies in a shilling or a 'bob' (which comprised two tanners or four thruppeny joeys) and twenty shillings in a pound or a 'quid' and twenty-one in a guinea. If you are under fifty don't even try to understand all this.

Gillings the grocer gave us twenty-four farthings for the sixpence. You couldn't do much with these tiny coins except lay them on the railway line and then try to pass them off as half pennies. But by distributing twenty-four coins in collection boxes, into poor men's hats and into puzzled children's hands we accomplished enough good deeds in one hour to give us the next fourteen days off.

THE GIRLS OF ST JOHN AND HOW TO DO THE TWIST

As seasoned Boy Scouts, we perceived few rivals when it came to other people in uniform. And, of course, in those days everybody, and not just meter readers, wore uniforms. There was the Army, Navy and Air Force just for a start. There was the Boys' Brigade, who took lofty vows and scrubbed their fingernails and, I suspect, washed behind their ears. The Boy Scouts also took vows but I don't recall us being so solemn. Even when we saluted we did so with only three fingers. But the Boys' Brigade would march around seriously singing 'We are the boys of the Boys Brigade'. Far out it was.

And then there was the St John Ambulance Brigade whose members knew how to set bones and carry survivors from weekend friendlies over their shoulders like sacks of potatoes. The St John girls were delightful. They wore grey skirts and white blouses and white gloves and affected our minds. But the boys were something else. Boy Scouts could also set bones of course - and not too badly either: a quick tug here, a bit of a twist there, a click and hey Bisto! We could also do the fireman's lift and used it once or twice on old ladies who were slow crossing busy roads.

In our perceptions of other people in uniform we recognised no superiors except perhaps the Royal Marine Commandos and Fighter Command.

We, of the Yellow Six, kept our chins up through those grim years of the 1940s when, because of food shortages, we were often forced (as I might have mentioned already) to eat our crusts. Some people might think that our sometimes daily fare of boiled carrots and cabbage was tantamount to suffering but that can only mean they know nothing of English cooking. Boiled vegetables come quite high on England's list of culinary delights.

English cooking has never been elaborate and, certainly, earning one's cooking badge in the Scouts was not too difficult. The most imaginative thing we made was 'twist'. One begins by mixing flour and water into a sort of Plasticine-like dough that can be rolled into a long, finger-thick worm. This is then wound, snake-like, around a green stick so that it can be turned over red hot coals. And that's it. *Oila*! as a French chef would say. That's twist.

Nowadays it's different. Scouts, before they go off to international jamborees, have to learn to prepare national dishes. This would hardly faze the French of course. They have to roast a *canard a l'orange* or do a *filet de boeuf Richelieu* to gain their cooking proficiency badge (second class); nor would it faze the Italians who can grill a *bistecca alla Fiorentina* while pitching a tent; or the Hungarians who learn to cook a *klasszikus gulyasleves* before they are out of the Wolf Cubs. I just hope the international scouting body has learned to make an exception of the English because, to entertain foreigners with English cooking is like trying to entertain a ladies' flower club with an exhibition of burping.

The Girls of St John and How to do the Twist

When the Yellow Six took part in the first big 'jamborette' after the war we were told by our scoutmaster, Thistlethwaite, how to prepare a traditional English recipe in case any foreign scouts were stupid enough to want to eat it. (I suppose the word 'prepare' is a little pretentious. So, in fact, is 'recipe'.) In any event, Thistlethwaite had a fairly low opinion of our cooking abilities and of our dining habits. Eating with the Yellow Six, he said, was tantamount to joining a chimpanzees' tea party, only less predictable. We were greatly flattered by this.

It took us ten minutes to learn how to boil cabbage and lumps of this and that. And we half came to grips with learning how to make custard which, we knew, went nicely with almost anything and was good to fall back on (so to speak) if one had unexpected guests. Thus, drooling and slobbering, we earned our cooking proficiency badges with flying custard and were ready to entertain the French, our main targets.

BEING NICE TO THE FRENCH

The 90 year old Boy Scouts movement was one of the first 'green' movements in the world and one of its many laudable ideals for outdoor behaviour - to leave nothing behind but one's footprints - remains a valid and important message. I must confess, here and now, and with whatever regrets may be necessary, that the Yellow Six never did achieve any recognisable level in outdoor pursuits or camping skills. We loved the outdoors nevertheless, and to this day you can probably still spot all the places where we camped.

In 1946, for a reason nobody ever fathomed, the Yellow Six was invited to take part in the first post-war international 'jamborette', which was on Cannock Chase in Staffordshire, not far from Streetly. We were allocated a small roped-off area on a grassy slope. It wasn't because of any prejudice against us or because Laidlaw and Arbuckle had boils. Every contingent was roped off.

Within our demarcated area we had to pitch our tent, light our camp fire and erect a flag pole. Because of the way the alphabet goes our site fell in between one allocated to Denmark and another to France and it overlooked a deep, dark woodland which filled us with fear. Many things filled us with fear, but particularly dark places because, during the war, as far as we were concerned, the dark was full of spies hoping to overhear some careless talk about the movement of His Majesty's battleships or the whereabouts of the Sixth Division or where the Yellow Six was hiding its latest ball of silver paper.

Our tent was extraordinarily large and heavy, being an ex-British Army job bought for a song at the Army and Navy Store on the periphery of Birmingham's bombed-out Bull Ring. The man told us it had belonged to Field-Marshal Bernard Montgomery and that it was bullet proof. Erecting it took hours and great co-ordination and much shouting and sometimes squabbling. Halfway through erecting it the French contingent, having long ago completed their astonishingly neat camp, and themselves looking insufferably antiseptic and neat, came to watch us. We had been told to be extra nice to the French because they were still a bit shell-shocked, and because of *Entente Cordiale* (which we thought must be a special French fruit drink and, if we were nice, they would share some with us).

We shouted jolly things to them in dreadful French but, halfway through getting our tent up, one of the French sniggered and our *bonhomie* snapped like a perished guy rope. Laidlaw, who knew some German, shouted at them in that language but with such an exaggerated guttural accent, and with so much goose-stepping, that it brought World War II flooding back in vivid Technicolor and Stereophonic Sound.

The French fell back. As they did so, the Welsh Kid (whom, it must be remembered, we let join the Yellow Six to demonstrate our level of cultural tolerance) shouted after them in Welsh, for quite a long time. He might have been a small kid but he had a very large mouth and, for some distance around, all dropped what they were doing to listen, enraptured because, although they could sense the richness of the language, they had no clue what language it was. Nobody had.

Nobody, that is, except the camp commanding officer, district commissioner Lieutenant Colonel Sir Llewellyn Llywarch-Griffiths. I was the first to notice Sir Llewellyn. I was, at the time, face down in the grass, retrieving some jam which we had spilled and I became aware of a shiny brown shoe a few inches from my face. Next to it was a second and matching brown shoe. From each shoe arose a very straight sock topped by a knobbly knee. As I raised my eyes I could see a pair of well-ironed military shorts and a shirt bearing so many medal ribbons it looked like a stamp album page filled with foreign stamps. Above the shirt was the splendid mustachioed head of the colonel.

Sir Llewellyn, visibly shaken by the tirade, reminded us that the Scout Law said 'A Scout is clean in thought, word and deed' and everybody looked at the Welsh Kid. The chief lambasted us for some minutes and even Laidlaw began to shuffle his feet uncomfortably. When he had done, Sir Llewellyn, with unnecessary emphasis, wiped his feet before stepping over the rope into the French Scouts' space.

We lost many points because of this episode, but we made a small fortune in sweets traded for translations of what the Welsh Kid had said.

The business about leaving nothing but footprints was serious stuff. Take, for example, the camp fire: one had to dig up a table-sized piece of turf, roll it up neatly like a Swiss roll, and store it. What never ceased to amaze me was that some scouts actually managed to do this. The idea was that when the camp was struck, we would rake the ashes flat and replace the grass. Hey Prestik! Not a trace of Man. But there were many nauseating traces of Boy. Apart from a large area of fire-blackened grass at our site there was porridge everywhere. For some reason, our porridge never seemed to biodegrade. Neither, we noticed, did it attract ants or other creatures. In fact it killed grasshoppers which were unfortunate enough to land in it. It was, Laidlaw pointed out, the same with our stews. One night we offered some stew to the French as a token of appeasement but they drove us off. We noticed though that they went quite green whenever they saw us cooking and Laidlaw said this was because they envied our cuisine.

We glowed. We thought cuisine was French for linguistics.

THE ART OF PREPARING CHITLINGS

I should explain that in the 1940s red meat was practically unobtainable and so we developed a taste for offal. My mother used to stuff an ox heart and bring it to the table with all the ceremony she might have reserved for a turkey.

And then there were chitlings.

My father had been asked by the Roberts family in Besom House, across the road from us, to slaughter a pig because the Robertses did not know how and Mr Roberts was away in the Royal Navy having a good time on the Murmansk convoys. The Robertses should have asked my mother - she could have killed a full grown landrace boar with one of her looks. My father, a Cockney and still quite new to village life, thought it a rather macho assignment, so off he went with a sharpened knife. We did not follow but stood in silence exchanging glances.

The scene that followed, I imagine, properly belongs to a horror movie. All I am prepared to say is that the hideous squeals and grunts we heard coming from across the road could not all have been coming from the pig. The long and short of it was that the Robertses rewarded my father with the chitlings - a bucket full of bowels.

The smell as my blood-soaked father entered the house was very agricultural and the job fell upon me to clean out a kilometre of intestine. I found the sphincter and slipped it over the kitchen tap holding it on tightly with both hands. My elder sister then turned the tap on.

The Yellow Six

The Art of Preparing Chitlings

As the water progressed along the transparent, elastic pipe - for that is what a pig's bowels are - so the tubing grew fatter and longer and longer, like an endless, transparent pink snake writhing sensuously. You could see all the little brown bits swirling along inside. Within seconds the first few metres of bowels had expanded to fill the kitchen sink but there were hundreds of metres still to go. I did not dare let go my end because the tap was on full. I shouted for my sister to turn the tap off but it was at this stage she panicked and ran from the house making for the high ground around Barr Beacon and calling upon everybody to follow.

The great pythonic loops now began to rise out of the sink and slither to the floor.

Phhhhthhhhaah!

The water had reached the pipe's northern end and now it began to whiplash around the kitchen floor like an unattended fireman's hose. Ah, the squeals and grunts that followed; the shouting and the weeping; the scrubbing and the disinfecting; the days of accusations and counter accusations; the action replays.

My mother then boiled the lot in an iron pot and left it to congeal into a grey fatty block. Then she sliced it up and, so help me, we ate it.

FANYANA AND THE BANANAS

One of the stunning things we learned during the war was that the world was not only round but that it had other countries filled with people stranger even than the Welsh.

As the Allied invasion of Europe drew near we watched in fascination the overseas contingents arriving, most of them wearing shoulder flashes describing their country of origin just like one saw on tins of pineapple or imported packets of dried bananas. One Sunday, while we were on patrol in Sutton Park, ambling through the heather crying 'peewit!' to disguise our presence, we stumbled across a black soldier lying in the grass muttering to a lady.

Unwittingly, we surrounded him, and he looked up at us with a strained expression. He smiled though, revealing an enormous array of gleaming white teeth. Instinctively we knew this was no American. For a start his uniform was of the heavy British quality. The lady, who spent some time straightening her skirt, surveyed all six of us, one by one, with unfriendly eyes.

The soldier sat up and we read 'Gold Coast' on his shoulder tabs. He told us the Gold Coast was in Africa and thus I had my first real contact with Africa. We knew all about Africa, of course - Tarzan and Jane, man-eating lions and Dr Livingstone who found the place. The soldier - I remember to this day that his name was Twumasi from Kumasi where bananas grew on trees - gave us the address of his young brother saying he was also a Boy Scout and we should write to him.

Fanyana and the Bananas

When we told Thistlethwaite about this he became very excited and told us about the Empire and how most of Africa was owned freehold by England because the English had found it first. He said we must write to Fanyana Twumasi and send him greetings on behalf of 1st Streetly as well as the Great White King. Although I saw little point in sending greetings (after all, what on earth can one do with greetings - even from a great white king?) I nevertheless wrote:

Dear Fanyana,

What a funny name you have. I suppose this is because you are black. How are you? I am a scout and so we have to talk to people of all races. You must have the same problem. We have a Welsh kid in our mist. We don't care, we are not too proud. Sometimes he behaves just like one of us.

I send greetings from the 1st Streetly and the Great White King, please find. I have a dog named Mugger, a pet rat named Macdonald, a snail which I am training to jump, and also two sisters.

It is raining as per usual and so I have nothing better to do than to write a letter. With luck it will snow. I don't suppose you get much snow in the jungal. We met your brother in the grass talking to a lady and he says you eat bananas all day. Here we queue up for just one banana each, twice a year. Chizz.

Have either of your parents been eaten by anything in Africa? Anything interesting I mean. Or your sister maybe?

Can you send me a spear with blood on it? I must close now because my mother says I must clean my room. Chizz. I hope you find my greetings. Yours truly.'

I recall his reply quite vividly it contained some perfunctory information about his family, none of whom had been eaten, and it contained a picture of him. He looked old, seventeen at least, and he had so many muscles he looked like a shiny bunch of black grapes. He ended by saying:

Fanyana and the Bananas

I like the Bible, please send me a Bible. I collect pictures of the blessed Virgin Mary. Please send holy pictures. I play soccer but haven't got a soccer ball. Please send a soccer ball.

His signature, a ten minute flourish, was followed by a PS. 'Don't forget the soccer ball.'
There the correspondence died.

THE DAY THE BEASLEYS' HOUSE CAUGHT FIRE

One of the longer chapter headings in *Scouting for Boys* reads:
ACCIDENTS AND HOW TO DEAL WITH THEM:
PANIC - FIRE - DROWNING - RUNAWAY HORSE -
MAD DOG - MISCELLANEOUS.

The Mad Dog fascinated us, but the thought of running up against a Miscellaneous excited us even more. Being attached to the Church of England our troop had a direct line to heaven and we used it frequently to pray for a Miscellaneous. Only now, looking back as a wise old man, do I realise how God fell over Himself to oblige us with miscellanies galore but we just failed to recognise them.

We also pored over an illustration in the book which showed a dismembered body flying through the air - it was a man who had carelessly used a candle to find a gas leak. The unsympathetic caption reads 'Bits of a silly ass'. As I was from London where 'ass' was pronounced 'arse' I was often invited to read the caption out loud, upon which the listeners would fall about because saying 'arse' in the Midlands was a mouth-washing offence.

A section in this chapter read 'House on Fire!' and it began with three 'musts':

1 Alarm the people inside. (sic)
2 Warn the nearest policeman or fire station.
3 Rouse neighbours to bring ladders, mattresses and carpets.

The Day the Beasleys' House Caught Fire

We often dreamt of finding a house on fire. The Germans, of course, did what they could to oblige but, alas, we weren't allowed to run about at night and, in any event, when a high explosive bomb hits a house there tended to be no need to alarm the occupants.

But soon after the war the Beasleys' house in the valley caught fire. It was on a Sunday morning and the amount of smoke coming from the back of the house and rising high above the trees was very dramatic. I was down there like a shot and found Vincent Laidlaw already there. Laidlaw had learned of the fire from his policeman father.

We both agreed there was no need to alarm the occupants because they were already nicely alarmed, and there was no need to tell the police because Laidlaw's father knew. I was glad Laidlaw's father was not there because, like all policemen, whenever the Yellow Six swung into action he would be obstructive. The nearest fire station was in distant Sutton Coldfield so people were taking it upon themselves to drag the Beasleys' furniture from the stricken house. Mrs Beasley was wailing and wailed louder and louder the more we tried to help.

I said that seeing the first two 'musts' were already attended to we had only to see to number three 'Rouse neighbours to bring ladders, mattresses and carpets'. So we ran around the neighbourhood getting carpets and ladders. As I have observed before that one tends to think clearly only AFTER such emergencies. The ladders turned out to be useless because the Beasleys' house was a bungalow. The carpets - for rolling people into if they should catch fire - were also a bit superfluous because none of the Beasleys caught alight. We asked Hazel, their daughter, if she would like us to roll her up in a carpet just for safety's sake, but she threatened to smash our heads.

Only when we had dragged most of the stuff out of the house and were thumbing through the Beasleys' magazines and looking at their wedding photographs did we notice there was no more smoke. It turned out that it was the Beasleys' stove which had caught alight.

At least the Beasleys ended up with more carpets and ladders than before the fire.

THE MOTHER OF ALL FIRES

On May 7 1945, after five and a half years of war and bombing and black out, the people of Britain were able to turn their lights on without first blacking out all their windows with special black out screens. Motorists were able to remove the masks from their headlights (only a narrow slit of light had been allowed on vehicles for all those years), and shops were able to light up their window displays.

The BBC played Vera Lynn singing 'When the lights go on again all over the world', incessantly, until people threatened to tear down Broadcasting House leaving not a stone upon a stone, but at least the children suddenly realised what the words of the song meant.

For most of our lives, up until that point, we had known only total darkness at night, relieved from time to time by the red glow on the horizon from burning buildings during air raids, the strobe-like flashes of anti-aircraft guns and the probing searchlight beams. We were brought up to view lights at night as a threat to our lives. One silly mistake, like turning on one's bedroom light without closing the curtains, could bring Dorniers and Heinkels roaring over from Berlin to bomb your house flat.

We were the first kids in history to be afraid of both the light and the dark.

On the day the Germans surrendered there was indescribable excitement at our end of the village. Flags and bunting appeared everywhere, along with pictures of Montgomery and Churchill. Schools were closed.

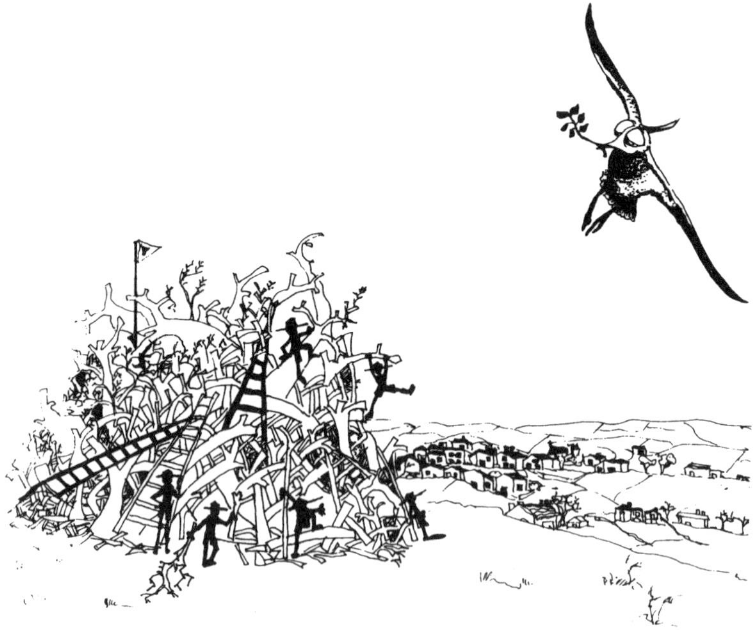

The Mother of All Fires

The children at our end of the village decided to light a huge bonfire and Haynes, the owner of One Hundred Acre Wood - the big silver birch and oak woodland at the west end of Streetly - allowed us to collect large amounts of dead wood, in fact whole trees. The Yellow Six, armed with axes and saws, swung into action chopping and sawing trees and collecting unwanted blackout screens and anything that was combustible.

In the field next to the wood we built the mother of all bonfires.

It was a magnificent structure, a work of architecture as well as engineering. People have received knighthoods for less heroic edifices. It was so high we had to borrow ladders to climb to the top so we could add even more stuff.

From every kitchen in the village arose the most delicious aromas - apple pies, rabbit and chicken pies, fairy cakes, pancakes. One ton of hoarded rations were whipped up, kneaded, mashed, stirred, mixed, blended, boiled, baked, fried and taken in solemn procession to the Great Fire where trestle tables had been set up.

Salivating freely, we could barely wait for dark, and, in the painfully slow dusk the lights went on all the way down Foley Road. People left their curtains open and some even found coloured globes to light outside their homes. As darkness fell we noticed an eerie white glare in the sky to the south - it was Birmingham all lit up.

We were awestruck and worried our eyeballs would dry out and crack.

More and more villagers began to troop up the rise and gather around the towering bonfire. The question arose, who should have the honour of lighting it?

As L*E*A*D*E*R of the Yellow Six it seemed only natural that as we had built the bonfire I should apply the first match. Laidlaw said as he had done most of the physical labour he should have the honour. The Welsh Kid said the village constable should. He could be a bit of a creep, could the Welsh Kid. I could see Thistlethwaite was dying to light it himself. So was the vicar, and the grocer who had given so many wooden boxes.

Everybody was now fingering match boxes when, suddenly, woosh! Somebody had tossed a match round the back of the fire.

A great beacon of light sprang into the night lighting up the Staffordshire/Warwickshire countryside and drowning out the stars. People oohed and aahed.

It was a pity about the ladders. I thought Laidlaw had removed them.

We had never seen so much food and beer in one place. We had never heard so much adult noise. Few people living outside England appreciate how festive the English can get. I saw a woman with Union Jack bloomers and a man without a tie. Somebody began singing in a high falsetto, 'There'll always be an England' and, just as we got to the part about 'Britons awake!' the air raid sirens began wailing. Everybody stopped in mid frolic. My mother said to my father, 'It's typical of the Germans! I told you they weren't at all happy about signing that unconditional surrender thing.'

My father, who was still an air raid warden, scoffed. 'It's a practical joke,' he said.

One or two other members of the ARP came over and my mother harangued them. 'Do your duty!' she cried.

Somebody murmured 'suicide bombers' and the phrase caught on. 'Put the fire out!' somebody yelled. 'They'll aim at it!' But nobody did, first because the fire could not be extinguished and, second, because we would have killed them.

The sirens persisted.

My father and two of his colleagues marched off into the night and we saw them, dimly, skirting the end of the wood and swinging into Foley Road. As they did so, somebody, allied, no doubt, to the practical jokers who had turned on the sirens, and who had been lurking within the depths of the wood, let off three war-issue thunder flashes.

'They've been shot!' somebody shouted.

My mother said: 'Who's for fresh pancakes?'

The war had hardened us all.

FENNING'S FEVER CURE

The wonderful thing about my career as a Boy Scout was that despite our positively septic habits we were rarely ill and this I put down to our robust outdoor life and Fenning's Fever Cure.

As children we contracted a fair variety of interesting illnesses, but none of them laid us low for long - scabies, verrucae, sties, ringworm, impetigo, nits, gingivitis... What has happened to all these diseases I wonder? Our mothers treated them all with bicarbonate of soda. Unless we fractured a leg in three places we never got to see a doctor. My mother had a thing about doctors and refused to see one even when she was heavy with child.

One day when, unbeknown to us, my mother was due to give birth, she simply sent me and my sister into the fields at the bottom of the garden and when we came back I found I had another confounded sister. My mother said she had dug it up from the cabbage patch. Looking at the new arrival I could see no reason to doubt this.

But Fenning's - that was something else. If you are under fifty you'll know nothing of Fenning's Fever Cure although Fenning still makes less unpleasant medicines. Today you wouldn't even offer Fenning's Fever Cure to a sick tree. When your mother approached with Fenning's - which smelled and tasted like battery acid - you would scream and cry until you were hoarse, but, under the lash, you'd be forced to swallow it even though it burned smoking holes wherever it spilled. When, next day, your mother asked after your health, you would say you were just fine, in fact absolutely marvellous, and you'd say you must get to school because

The Yellow Six

you felt this terrible thirst for knowledge. 'Knowledge! Knowledge!' you would cry as you dragged yourself from the house and then waded through waist-deep snow for ten kilometres in a howling blizzard.

Anything rather than Fenning's.

What happened to Mr Fenning? I often lay awake wondering. Did some child, on reaching adulthood, hunt him down, chloroform him, tie him to a chair in an abandoned barn and force him to drink bottles of his own fever cure until he begged to be clubbed to death?

I hope so.

Fenning's Fever Cure

DANCING AND LOOKING AFTER ONE'S OWN CHITLINGS

Personal hygiene and maintaining good general health are important in the Boy Scouts. And although the title of the Boy Scouts' bible, *Scouting for Boys*, in today's context, sounds like the title of a racy book for hungry young women, it is in fact a book of singular virtue, as innocent as Peter Pan and filled with good advice.

In his chapter, 'How to Grow Strong', Baden-Powell says: 'When I was a fairly active young bounder I went in for skirt dancing.' As I feared, the dictionary defines skirt dancing as 'dancing with long, flowing skirts'. Baden-Powell says it amused his regimental comrades and was good exercise.

I say!

He then describes how dancing prepared him for when he was 'on service against the Matabele' - i.e. shooting Zulus. He was sometimes chased by them for the Zulu never did play fair.

'I found myself outdistancing my pursuers with the greatest of ease because of my foot management gained in skirt dancing.'

The Yellow Six would rather the Matabele had caught us, and run us through with rusty assegais, than have put on a skirt and danced. It was this vision of grown men dancing in long skirts that put me off ballroom dancing even in later youth. ('Now, young man, unless we let go of the door handle, we can't learn how to dance, can we?')

Another quaintness in *Scouting for Boys* is that Baden-Powell found it difficult to talk about, well... you know, um... well, about one's own

Dancing and Looking After One's Own Chitlings

personal chitlings. He said that to be strong you had to be clean inside as well as outside and this meant 'having a rear, daily, without fail'. A rear? He can't mean a... he does! He means to evacuate the chitlings. To have a chitling movement. And he goes on to give jolly good advice about exercising one's chitlings.

One must also exercise the mind, he says. Here one must make up one's own rules... using your frontal lobe do twenty-five press-ups. Now, push your thumbs into your ears and pinch your nose between your pinky fingers; shut your mouth tightly and blow, forcing air upwards into the cranium. Feel your mind expand? Now let the air escape, explosively, through your ears, thus clearing out the wax.

One of the mental exercises we used to do was sit in a circle round our scoutmaster, Thistlethwaite, who would read Baden-Powell's 'Heroic Stories'. One I especially recall was about a Boy Scout who, though lame, tried to rescue a little girl 'playing on the railway line at Clydebank in front of an approaching train'. Both were killed.

We often debated this: what would we have done in similar circumstances? I thought anybody who played on the railway in front of approaching trains would have been a write off, sooner or later, and certainly it would not be worth putting Segs in their shoes to make them last. Risk your life rescuing such a girl - and what is to say that, next day, she doesn't go wheeling her doll's pram along the M1? Laidlaw said he would have lassoed her.

Baden-Powell gives advice on what to do about bigger girls. 'Don't,' he said, 'lark about with a girl with whom you would not like your mother or sister to see you.' Here we would all nudge each other and say grown-up things like 'Pssshaw!'until Thistlethwaite gave us a look.

But what took the cake was this advice 'FAIR PLAY - if you see a big bully going for a small weak boy, you stop him because it is not "fair play". And if a man, in fighting another, knocks him down, he must not hit or kick him while he is down; everybody would think him an awful beast if he did.'

'Like hell,' Laidlaw would murmur. Oh, we were such bounders.

HOW THE SPRING WAS SPRUNG

The English never talk about the weather except in tones more appropriate to a superstitious tribe discussing how to appease the spirits lurking within a nearby hyperactive volcano. And no Englishman, in his right mind, would say 'It's not going to rain today'. It would precipitate rain as surely as some more scientific method such as seeding the clouds with CO_2 crystals, or planning a garden party.

Frankly, I did not subscribe to these superstitions. I just accepted the fact that the British are pathologically unable to forecast weather just as they cannot cook. One simply has to recall the coronation of Queen Elizabeth in 1953 when the British Government called in its most experienced weather forecasters to determine the day of the year on which rain would be least likely to fall. They said June 2 and so the Coronation took place on the wettest day London experienced that summer. Nine years previously, also in London, the Supreme Headquarters, Allied Expeditionary Force, had called in top experts to determine the day on which the English Channel would be at its calmest for the D-Day landings. The weathermen said it would be June 5. On June 5 gale-force winds lashed the Channel while the rain, flying horizontally, soaked all those seasick soldiers in landing barges. D-Day had to be postponed for twenty-four hours.

About the time I was taking my meteorological proficiency badge and learning how to speak frankly and openly about the weather, my maternal grandmother came to stay. She was *very* superstitious about talking of the weather.

'Never speak of Spring,' she said. 'Just be thankful if you get one, but pretend you have not noticed it.'

She was terribly old (fifty I shouldn't wonder) and looked like Hagar. I would never have said this to her face, you understand, or she would have gored me. She claimed that if you said out loud that you could smell Spring, the warm, gentle breeze which had borne the scent of daffodils would suddenly become a howling north-easter, snap-freezing people in mid-posture as they bent to tie their laces or raised an arm to hail a cab.

It was the winter of '42 that my grandmother, irritated by the recent Blitz and now unnerved by the quietness following the temporary cessation of bombing raids on London, took refuge in our house in Streetly. She was, to our unspeakable relief, about to go home when it snowed and snowed for weeks.

In January we became paralysed under deep snow. We could leap out of the upper storey bedroom windows into it. The telephone lines became coated with ice until they were the diameter of broomsticks - and then they snapped. At night we were awakened by the sound of huge branches breaking off trees under the weight of snow.

Streetly was ten kilometres east of our school in the direction of Siberia, and so school became unreachable. We were trapped at our end of the village and forced to amuse ourselves by setting upon anybody smaller or weaker than ourselves. Finally the Army sent a tank squadron to compact a route through to us so that emergency medical supplies of Fenning's Fever Cure and beer for the ARP could be rushed in.

The commander of a tank asked my sister and me which way the road went (the snow was so deep one could not tell) and we, not wanting the tanks to churn up our toboggan run, managed to direct him through the Hardcastle's snow-buried greenhouse. We sent a second tank into an ancient cesspit. My sister said, if we wrote to the Germans, they would give us Iron Crosses for what we had done.

Towards February the weather warmed up and to celebrate what appeared to be the beginning of the thaw, and the fact that Grandma would now be able to return to London while the Germans still had a

How the Spring was Sprung

chance to get her, we rolled a huge snow ball. As we rolled it, it cleared a track exposing the grass so long hidden, dank and yellow from lack of light. But in among the tousled grass I discovered a single crocus whose purple flower was, miraculously, partly opened and whose leaves were a rich green. It was as if it knew something we did not. I picked it and, feeling like Noah's dove returning to the Ark bearing an olive branch to indicate land was near, I slapped the crocus on the kitchen table.

'Spring is here!' I said.

Next day nothing could move in the whole of Britain and Europe and east as far as Pyongyang. The Germans became snowbound on the Eastern Front, enabling the Russians to consolidate their recent gains; Axis supplies to the Western Desert ground to a halt on German railways and thus the Eighth Army stormed into Tunisia.

That blizzard, said Churchill (not to me, mark you), changed the course of the war.

My grandmother hitched a ride out of our village on a tank, never to return.

THE GRAND PRIX

I heard in 1993 that the 1st Streetly, now a strong troop, had celebrated its 50th anniversary with a Grand Prix Celebration Camp which, I gathered, was a test of camping skills and outdoor elegance.

Camping skills? Ha! The Yellow Six would have cleaned up. They would have forced us to.

As for a Grand Prix...

In the Summer of 1947 the Boy Scouts Association's divisional headquarters announced a *real* grand prix - a grand scale soap box derby. The Yellow Six decided to enter.

A soap box derby is simply a downhill race for free-wheeling carts which we referred to as trolleys. The Scouts had a tradition for soap box derbies and the trolleys we made often displayed mechanical genius. The pilots of some of these machines displayed the sort of courage that made Britain great. Other skills were necessary too, larceny for instance.

The trolley we assembled in 1947 was made possible only by Bodley-Smith removing, on a temporary basis let it be said, the wheels from his baby sister's pram, which was one of those regal conveyances with huge front wheels and little rear ones. We reversed this arrangement and placed the large wheels at the rear of our trolley - a design innovation which was to become shamelessly copied by drag racing car designers the world over.

We called our trolley the Yellow Streak and we chose the bleak heights of Barr Beacon, above the west end of Streetly, for its test

The Yellow Six

run. Beacon Hill begins with a sudden steep descent - a stomach dislodging drop - and goes into a long, fast, 1.5 km gradient along Foley Road to end in abrupt collision with cat flattening Chester Road traffic. The Beacon itself is the highest point from there to the Ural Mountains in Russia. When the north-east wind blows it comes straight off the Steppes causing one's teeth fillings to shrink and drop out.

Bodley-Smith was given the honour of piloting our machine. No sooner was he seated than it rocketed away down the hill. Many watchers covered their eyes. Some fainted.

We all agreed afterwards that Bodders did from 0-100 km/h in three seconds. He himself recalled nothing except feeling terribly cold. This could be because halfway down the hill he hit a bump which caused the Yellow Streak to soar to a height where, I fancy, it probably passed through the high altitude jetstream blowing off the Siberian tundra. He then performed a slow motion victory roll followed by a barrel roll and, finally, re-entry - clean through the Turberville's much admired yew hedge which, up to that instant, was a fine example of olde English topiary.

THE OLYMPIAD

One of the last great achievements of the Yellow Six under my leadership was in 1948 when the first post-war Olympiad was staged in London. The Boy Scouts Association encouraged Scout troops to hold their own local indoor Olympics. The games suggested were not very masculine, in fact they were decidedly wet, and so we decided to invent our own. After all, had we not, only three years previously, turned the tide of war for the Allied Nations by collecting silver paper and old saucepans? And had we not saved the Chinese from starving by single mindedly eating our crusts? (Answers can be obtained by writing to the British War Museum.)

Then one of the new-fangled scoutmasters - usually fairly recently demobbed army officers - asked how we could stage an Olympiad without international participation? We pointed to the Welsh Kid. Our international status could not be questioned.

We announced the Games around the village and, although nobody but a few scouts turned up, we opened the Streetly Olympiad with an elaborate and moving flag-raising ceremony with much saluting, bugling and naked Olympic flames.

We had athletics, wrestling, long-distance spitting and other events - all of which Laidlaw won. Then we organised a helping-old-ladies-across-the-street event for which we lured old Mrs Winterbotham into the Scout Hall. She was slightly senile. For this event Arbuckle pretended to be a double decker bus and, making roaring noises, rushed up and down the Scout Hall while we took turns in hurrying Mrs Winterbotham from one side to the other.

The Olympiad

Bodley-Smith won the getting-a-stone-out-of-the-horse's-hoof event for which we used a pig's trotter. Afterwards we boiled the pig's trotter and, in an emotional ritual, ceremoniously ate it.

We let Mrs Winterbotham go.

THE GANG SHOW

The Olympiad was not our first public performance. Our first was a Gang Show.

In November 1944, when the war was going quite well for the Allies, Thistlethwaite's brother, Percy, came home on leave from Ensa, the entertainment arm of the British forces. Percy had the rank of major and Thistlethwaite - obviously anxious to smarten us all up - told us that Major Thistlethwaite would like to review the entire 1st Streetly Troop and so we must all come next week in freshly pressed uniforms and with our hat brims ironed flat.

We must also arrive with a minimum amount of stuff in our pockets, he said, giving Arbuckle one of his Meaningful Looks. Arbuckle, whose uniform bulged all over like a sack of potatoes, was famed for carrying in his pockets more than most people could stuff into the boot of a car. He carried almost anything one could ever need for almost any conceivable occasion. The Boy Scout motto is 'be prepared' and if there had been a prize for the most prepared scout in Britain, Arbuckle would have won it.

We once needed a spanner to fix somebody's bike and from the depths of Arbuckle's left trouser pocket came one of those multi-purpose cycle spanners. One of his best efforts was when Thistlethwaite was telling us about cooking snails in a survival situation and Arbuckle fished from this same left pocket two aestivating snails which, curiously, Thistlethwaite declined to cook. Arbuckle also carried enormous quantities of string and elastic bands; matches, a compass, notebook and pencil with pencil sharpener; he carried a German ten pfennig coin just in case the tide of war turned; he carried a pebble in case he ever had to go without water (sucking a pebble is somehow supposed to assuage one's thirst but I could never resist chewing it); he had a small electric motor; a dog lead, a tin of fish hooks and a length of line; he had a tiny dictionary, envelopes and a stamp.

This was just in his left trouser pocket.

Suspended from his belt was a very heavy scout knife with a collapsible fork and spoon, a saw, fish scaler, pliers and toothpick. As a result of all this cargo he had a wasp waist from having to pull his belt very tight to keep his trousers from crashing to the floor. Laidlaw asked him what would happen if he fell into deep water. He would surely go down like the *Bismarck*. Arbuckle said he carried an inflatable tube but he refused to show it.

We duly arrived for the Major's inspection, many of us having successfully walked or ridden from our homes without falling in puddles or even getting mud on our shoes. And we all stood at the 'alert' (Scouts don't use the command 'attention') in a line so straight we all kept bending forward to admire it.

The Major, bidding us all stand at ease, harangued us. He turned out to be a theatrical producer in civvy life and he told us of the morale-building role of the theatre on the battlefield as well as on the home front. I imagined for a long time afterwards that the dramatic music in war films was played by Ensa ensembles which followed soldiers into action to boost their morale. (General: 'I say, Major! I thought your choice of music for the Normandy landings a trifle - how shall I say? - inappropriate. Your choice of "Oh, I do like to be beside the seaside" was a little frivolous, don't you think?')

The Major told us how he and his brother, Rodney, had, the night before, thought of the idea of producing a Boy Scout 'Gang Show' so that the entire 1st Streetly Troop, which numbered about forty scouts, could put on a public performance and make some much needed funds. At the mention of our scoutmaster's first name we all began to titter because we had never heard it used before. Major Thistlethwaite motioned us to settle down before he continued.

Gang shows are peculiar to the Boy Scouts. They are, the Major explained, variety concerts specially designed by his friend, the great theatrical producer, Ralph Reader, for Boy Scouts. Each of us, he said, had a talent to entertain people whether we recognised it or not.

He then pointed to Bill Gunson of the Wolf patrol and said: 'You, my boy, what talent do you have that others find entertaining?' Gunson was the one scout who really did have a talent - he could play an amazing variety of tunes by placing his mouth against a hair comb covered by a piece of paper and then humming against it.

The Major said this was 'marvellous'.

He turned to Laidlaw who had obviously not been listening. 'And you?' he asked.

'What about me?' asked Laidlaw who was so startled he saluted and clicked his heels.

'What can you do that would entertain people?'

'Nothing, sir,' he said, clicking his heels again.

'Then you can be stage manager!' said the Major. I knew enough about Laidlaw and about amateur dramatics to know that the Major had made a tactical blunder on a par with Hitler's march into Russia.

When it came to my turn to answer I said, a little facetiously, that I could whistle. 'But that's splendid!' cried the Major. 'Can you whistle "Rule Britannia" for us?'

I then did so and everybody clapped. I had never been clapped before and I rather liked it. I began to think that maybe I had a theatrical career ahead of me as the Wonder Boy Whistler.

It was indeed amazing how many talents the forty of us had. No less than five boys could play the piano so, obviously, piano playing was easier than whistling. Several said they could sing; one could play the spoons - a singularly unmusical talent entailing clacking two spoons on the side of one's leg; two claimed their respective dogs could do tricks as in a circus and there was instant rivalry as each boasted of having taught his dog to do the most unbelievable things; another could make quite clever shadows appear on the wall by contorting his hands in front of a light; another could imitate birds.

Watson said he would paint a beach ball to make it look like a globe of the world and then mimic Charlie Chaplin who, in the classic 1940 film, *The Great Dictator*, pretended to be Adolf Hitler. In the movie, Chaplin bounced the 'World' on his head and executed several clever little back heels and got the ball to bounce off his knees and even off his bottom. Thistlethwaite thought this a 'super' idea.

We also learned a new trick one of us would walk on to the stage apparently carrying, single handedly, a stretcher with somebody lying on it and nobody holding up the other end. This was done by holding two scout poles horizontally, while a second scout pretended to be the victim. He walked in front of you, between the poles, with his head thrown back as if asleep. A sheet draped along the full length of the poles hid the fact that 'the patient' was actually walking while helping the stretcher bearer hold up the poles.

The Major then told us he and Rodney had drawn up a rough theatrical production and that the show would open with a patriotic tableau where the entire troop of forty boys would march on to the stage singing 'There'll always be an England' - including the Welsh Kid. I would whistle a solo.

We agreed to spend a weekend rehearsing.

There were to be lots of patriotic songs backed by music from a gramophone as well as flags and wartime sound effects. We even found ourselves a small air raid siren.

The Gang Show had the makings of a great evening. Equally, it had all the makings of a disaster.

It was during this period of my life that I first heard the expression 'It'll be all right on the night.' The Major used this expression more and more but, each time he did so, his voice seemed to rise higher and higher.

Came the night and a few dozen people filed into the Church Hall where they sat expectantly staring at the closed curtains. Laidlaw, in mid stage, held the curtains closed while forty boys jostled and pushed in the wings ready for the Grand March on to the stage.

At one point Laidlaw stuck his head through the curtains to see how the hall was filling up and it must have looked so ridiculous that the audience laughed. Embarrassed, Laidlaw hurriedly withdrew his head. But then he became so intoxicated by the laughter that he could not resist doing it again. And again. Now, the art of comedy is to know when to stop but nothing could stop Laidlaw.

Eventually the Major hissed to him to get back to the wings.

Laidlaw took this to be a command to open the curtains and did so before we were properly ready. The Major, sensing that nothing could stop us anyway, said 'Qui-eeek march!' and on we all trooped.

The Gang Show

The band was totally unprepared so the only music came from Gunson with his comb and paper.

Bewildered by the lack of supporting music Watson, when he reached mid stage, stopped dead in his tracks and everybody piled into him. Thistlethwaite, prompting from the wings, muttered 'There'll always be an England' and motioned us to strike up the song. So we abandoned the march-on pageant and began, raggedly at first, to sing 'There'll always be an England'. When the third verse came up and I was supposed to whistle it solo no sound would issue from my pursed lips, dry from nerves. This caused enormous mirth among the audience.

After the stage was cleared Watson was ushered back on with his inflated-globe-of-the-world-act - but he had not had time to paint on his little black Hitlerian moustache and his world, having sprung a fast leak, hung limply in his hand. The audience was totally mystified.

As for the two performing dogs, one was on heat and the pair mated happily in the middle of the stage ignoring all orders from their respective owners to play dead. At this stage the fretting Major said the Welsh Kid and I should go on stage with the stretcher trick and so divert attention from the dogs. As we walked on to the stage Laidlaw stood on the sheet and so we walked on without it - just two boys holding two poles.

This also clearly puzzled the audience.

The entire show descended into a lavish demonstration of what is usually called 'low comedy'. The only star of the show was 'FA Cup' Hayward (his nickname stemmed from the size of his ears) who played the piano so well he received encore after encore until the boy who was turning the pages of his sheet music 'accidentally' dropped the piano lid on Hayward's extraordinary long, thin fingers.

In the *grande finale* in which we all sang and played different kinds of instruments including some unlikely ones, Laidlaw wound up the air raid siren which, to our consternation, caused the entire audience to evacuate the hall.

They never came back.

THE SCOUT KNIFE AND MORE LITTLE OLD LADIES

Over the years I lost touch with the 1st Streetly Boy Scouts. This is not surprising seeing that we all went our separate ways never to communicate from that day to this.

But once you have been a Boy Scout you never really grow out of it. Even in middle age one retains an enthusiasm for the great outdoors and for climbing trees and walking in puddles - and for knives. Particularly knives.

Not too long ago a leaflet came in the post: 'Genuine Swiss Army knife - specially designed for the outdoor enthusiast. Ideal for Scouts.' I rushed home to ask my wife if I could have one.

'They say stocks are limited,' I called out as I carefully wiped my feet before entering the house. 'And it's only £19.99!' However, my natural honesty (another hangover from the Boy Scouts) led me to confess: 'Exc. VAT.'

She didn't hear. She was at the shops.

I pored over the advertisement. The knife, as illustrated, had all its blades and things opened out like an electrocuted porcupine. Apart from a Philips screwdriver, toothpick, tweezers and wire bender - all four of which had my outdoor enthusiast's mind pondering - the knife had eight other functions. It took me back to the days of the Yellow Six when I owned a Boy Scout knife. We considered these complicated enough but, in retrospect, each simply had a large blade for cutting one's finger and a spike which, as I have already described, was for getting stones out of horse's

The Scout Knife and More Little Old Ladies

hooves or old ladies on to buses. They weighed so much I had to wear mine chained to my waist because, suspended from the belt it dragged my pants down.

Some of us also carried sheath knives. Nowadays these are called 'survival knives' and can cost as much as the Third World debt. They have to be capable of holding an edge even after being used to prise open a bank safe, and must be sturdy enough to cut thick poles and hammer them into the ground to build a survival shelter with bathrooms *en suite*. In a survival situation (i.e. you haven't had water for seven days, your food has run out, you've lost your cake fork and you are in Africa being followed by a thin lion) your knife becomes your best friend.

You should be able to hammer the blade into a tree, for instance, so you can use it as a step to climb up and get away from some animal you might have irritated, or to reach fruit or birds' eggs. Some survival knives have a saw on one side of the blade capable of clearing a five hectare stand of mature Douglas firs in six minutes.

My scout knife was, for the 1940s, state of the art (as they would say today) and, in my heart of hearts, I know it was possession of this impressive knife that propelled me into the number one position in the Yellow Six as much as the training I received from my dog Mugger.

Later, all six of us acquired knives and when the *Luftwaffe* was daily letting more and more daylight into our lives we enthusiastically assisted the process by clearing wide areas with our knives. Take Four Oaks, near Sutton Coldfield - it used to be Nine Oaks.

My knife was eventually stolen and my mother maintained it must have been taken by an agent working for the National Trust.

(In case you are wondering, my wife eventually came home but said I could not have the knife and anyway what had happened to my Outdoor Enthusiast's Magnifying Glass with Imitation Ivory Handle which she had bought me for Christmas? I had to confess I had swapped it for an Outdoor Enthusiast's personal bleeper.)

THE END OF EVERYTHING

How did it all end?

By VE Day our shirts were smothered in proficiency badges for such things as fire lighting, bird watching, cooking... the cooking badge was, perhaps, a little more difficult than I have led readers to suppose. One earned it only if somebody held down what you had cooked, for five minutes - while smiling and whistling. This was later reduced to four minutes and is an indication of how standards had begun to slip.

The post-war period saw many returning ex-servicemen - men who had done real scouting in Africa and in the Far Eastern jungles - starting to run Boy Scout troops. I imagine the older men who had been running the troops were greatly relieved.

The new scoutmasters were heroes who had sometimes been shot down, or even up. They brought a new discipline to scout troops and made us do things we just weren't used to - like polish our shoes, cook food without messing and take part in cross-country hikes eating nothing until we were back at base which often meant going without food for up to an hour.

The good days were over.

To be frank, I fear for the future of the Scouts. This is not because of too much discipline but because of girls.

My sister's reactions during the chitlings crisis was a very good example of why the Boy Scouts in my day would not let girls in. It was not chauvinism. It was simply that girls can get in the way and are irrational and tend to criticise you when you do something dumb and when the last thing you want is for somebody to point it out in a high-pitched voice filled with pitiless scorn. Girls are the sort of people who peer under a bus at some poor fellow who has been run over and ask him why he didn't look where he was going.

They can smile but few of them can whistle.

Despite this, the Canadians, a few years ago, decided to admit girls and to abolish the name Boy Scouts. Now it is The Scouts. The move and its consequences rank along with Britain's relinquishing India and, eventually, the British Empire. The Yellow Six would never have tolerated such a move. Again, this was not because we were chauvinists. We helped old ladies across the road, didn't we? (Answer: Yes.) We were hardly even racist. Did we not allow a Welsh kid to join our ranks? (Answer: Verily.) And, as everybody in his heart of hearts knows, being non-sexist and non-racist is, in any society, almost impossible these days, especially so in societies where there are females and where there are people of different colours. But to have girls around when one is trying to do something that requires concentration, like light a fire with two matches, or open a jack-knife without laying open one's hand, is intolerable.

I have mentioned before that the Welsh Kid had a sister, Bronwyn. Bronwyn, who had flowing red hair, had the power to strike dumb the entire Yellow Six - just by smiling at us. If she spoke directly to one of us, that person would be unable to speak for nearly a week. If he opened his mouth, nothing would come out except, perhaps, a three week old wad of American Wrigley's chewing gum.

Girls were massively distracting.

In any event, between Thistlethwaite's dark hints about the dangers of letting our minds wander where girls were concerned, and Baden-Powell's book which warned (and still does so) about lascivious thoughts, we were ill-prepared for girls. We felt guilty whenever we saw one and, in our confusion, all but Laidlaw, would begin walking into trees and up against walls.

Laidlaw was the only worldly one among us. He had reached a point where he could actually 'chat up' girls. He would let his arms

The End of Everything

dangle loosely, push his scout hat back on his head and affect an American accent - and they all fell for it. He would say things like 'Hi!'

The point I want to make is that the Yellow Six, which carved a whole new chapter in British scouting history, was a fine, cohesive unit which could march in a straight line - until it discovered girls. That was the end of us. We slowly broke up, each member ambling off, mouth open, eyes crossed, hair carefully parted and slicked down, following a girl who never even bothered to look back over her shoulder.

ACKNOWLEDGEMENTS

Some of the characters in this book are based on real life but the scoutmaster, Thistlethwaite, is pure fiction. The 1st Streetly Boy Scouts Troop is, today, a thriving unit, I am told, and its members will be relieved to know that a lot of the incidents recounted here are . . . well, (how do I put this?) . . . somewhat exaggerated.

Some of the adventures in this book germinated in my daily humour column, Stoep Talk, in *The Star*, Johannesburg.

I owe thanks to my family for their forbearance, particularly my daughter Julie for her drawings and her suggestions; to my late mother, Anne Elizabeth Clarke of Streetly, for her help - although she claimed not to recognise a single fact in this book. She claimed she didn't even remember me. I am also grateful to my sisters - Ann Webb of Streetly who introduced me to my publisher, Alan Brewin of Brewin Books, and Victoria Withers of Erdington, Birmingham; the late Antony Llywarch of Guildford; Keith Crossley and Bob Saunders of the Boy Scouts Association in Johannesburg for helpful ideas; my brother-in-law, Boris Babaya of Johannesburg, for his critical reading of the manuscript and for his valuable suggestions;

But, above all, I owe a huge debt of gratitude to Richard Steyn, former Editor-in-Chief of *The Star* in Johannesburg, who persuaded me - a mostly serious science writer for 35 years - to write a daily humour column. The idea was to leaven the newspaper's grim contents during the violent days of South Africa's political metamorphosis. As a result I thoroughly enjoyed the revolution.

James Clarke
Sandton, Gauteng
South Africa

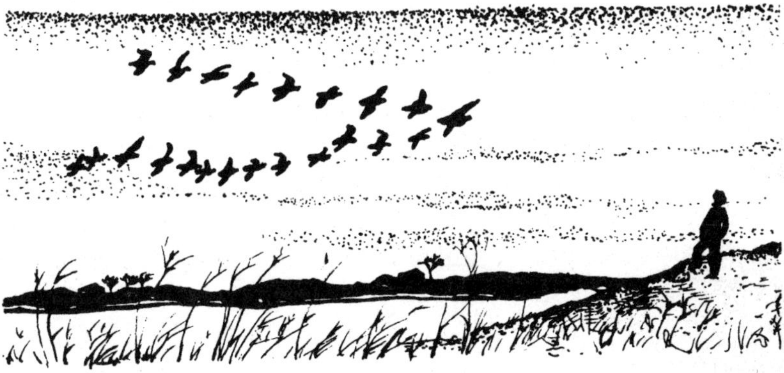